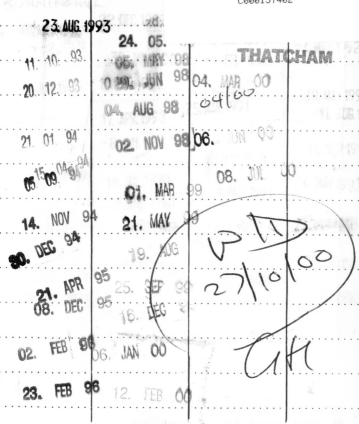

TRIVIAL DISPUTES

TRIVIAL DISPUTES

Fraser Harrison

Illustrated by Harriet Dell

COLLINS
8 Grafton Street, London W1
1989

William Collins Sons & Co. Ltd
London · Glasgow · Sydney · Auckland
Toronto · Johannesburg

BRITISH LIBRARY CATALOGUING IN PUBLICATION DATA

Harrison, Fraser, 1944–
Trivial disputes
1. Great Britain. Social life, 1945–1960.
Biographies
I. Title
941.085'092'4

ISBN 0–00–217856–7

First published 1989
Copyright © Fraser Harrison 1989
Set in Linotron sabon at the Spartan Press Ltd,
Lymington, Hants
Printed and bound in Great Britain
by William Collins Sons & Co. Ltd, Glasgow

To Harriet,
with much affection and admiration

ACKNOWLEDGEMENTS

I would like to express my warmest thanks to Helen Fraser for her creative influence, and for suggesting this book in the first place; to Maggie Hanbury for guiding my fortunes so affably; and to Ariane Goodman for her perceptive editorial advice. As always, I am very grateful to Sally for her support, which she gives unstintingly, and to Tilly and Jack, for being my favourite children. Finally, I would like to thank the present occupants of my old home in Liverpool for kindly allowing Harriet and me to see the house as it is today.

PROLOGUE

Standing on a chest of drawers in my parents' bedroom and dignified by a little silver frame is a photograph of the three of us. It must have been professionally taken, for we are all in our smartest clothes, and we have been carefully grouped and posed to achieve the effect of a formal family portrait. The mood of the photograph is, however, far from formal: my mother, in a dashing hat, smiles gaily, my father radiates the good cheer of a prospering young man blessed with a pretty wife, and I, a round-faced, fair-haired, snub-nosed, over-dressed child, sit between them, beaming hilariously. Like all family photographs, this one conceals as much as it reveals,

9

but it fascinates me for a special reason. Shortly after it was taken, I suffered a terrible accident which changed my appearance for ever, and it is therefore a portrait of someone I never became.

One afternoon, when I was three, my mother walked me to the shops at the end of our road, something she did almost daily. Like all small children, I enjoyed shopping expeditions, and I especially relished the chance to wheel out and fuss over my sizeable family of soft toys. The vehicle I used for this purpose had been a subject of contention. To my parents' embarrassment, I had clamoured that year to be given a pram for my birthday, and feeling that even the most robust pram would be too effeminate for a boy to be seen pushing, they had compromised by buying me a milk-float, which, as I recall, was painted a manly shade of blue. I was mightily pleased with it for other reasons: it was designed to be strong and practical and was fitted with two broad shelves to carry its load of toy milk bottles, but I jettisoned these at once, turning it into as fine a pram as any girl had ever boasted. Thus, at a stroke, honour and desire were perfectly satisfied. My family comprised a mixed bunch of animals and a single girl-doll, who was no risk to my reputation, for she had lost all signs of gender save a single stringy pigtail. My unchallenged favourite was a small, green, knitted elephant, whose velvet feet exuded a comforting ichor when sucked. And so it was that on this fateful afternoon I followed my mother along the pavement, pushing my acceptable milk-cart.

According to our custom, she went in and out of the shops that stood in a row along Booker Avenue and I stayed on the pavement outside tending to the needs of my menagerie. While she was in the grocery, I was approached by a real animal in the shape of a large, black Labrador. We had dogs of our own to which I was very attached, and I was confident in my relations with the dog population at large. I did not hesitate to reach out and stroke this one's muzzle, which was at much the same height as mine. Perhaps I was too abrupt in my movements, as small children often are, or perhaps I made an alarming noise, but whatever small provocation I may or may not have offered, the dog responded to my overture by burying its teeth in my face and virtually severing my nose.

I must have screamed, and the dog was no doubt growling as it attacked me. The scene attracted the attention of an old man, who hurried over and beat off the dog with his stick. He then fell on to the pavement himself. My mother ran out and picked me up, struggling to preserve what was left of my nose. She carried me into the chemist. The old man, meanwhile, was being carried into the next-door shop. My mother sat me on her knee, her hand to my face, my blood soaking both of us, and the chemist rang for an ambulance. My father was rung at his office.

An hour later, in the Children's Hospital in Myrtle Street, my mother, whose feelings may be imagined, was bluntly informed by the surgeon that the operation I was about to undergo was unlikely to be successful and that my chances of keeping a nose fit to be seen were small. By then I was on my way to the theatre.

I can only tell this part of the story in the baldest terms, for I have no memory of the experience. Not a single image or echo has lodged in my mind. I do have a vivid picture of the dog standing over me as I made to touch it, but thereafter the light goes out, and I can recall nothing of the hospital, either before or after the operation. The process of oblivion would appear to be functioning still, because although I have often heard my mother's version of these grisly events, which in such cases almost always stands in for authentic memory, I cannot retrieve even her words now that I come to write my own account.

In the event, the surgeon's prognosis turned out to be pessimistic. From a mechanical point of view, the operation was a triumph, for I was able to breathe easily through my reconstructed nose, and needed only one further small, though horrific, remedial operation ten years later. It is true that one nostril was left noticeably smaller than the other, and that as a child I suffered from chronic catarrh, but then so did most of the children who sucked their oxygen in the 'fifties from Liverpool's pungent and turbid atmosphere. As for my operation's aesthetic impact, I can only leave it to others to judge whether my nose is presentable to public gaze. Its proportions are certainly generous and it bears a pronounced skew to the left, but I come from a family of men who have been distinguished by noses of noble design, and while my father's is straight, my grandfather's nose shared with mine a conspicuous bias, also to the left, so I cannot distinguish the hereditary from the accidental. The surgeon, whose bedside manner may have been a little rough, was nonetheless an artist when it came to wielding his needle. Once my wounds had healed, I showed no more than the faintest, neatest scars on my upper lip, which today are virtually invisible. There was a time, during adolescence of course, when I was acutely conscious of my misshapen 'conk', as my father called it, but as a child I was never worried about it, and since adulthood I have taken a certain pride in my singular, unmistakable organ.

This episode must have left some psychological scars, I suppose, but as far as I can tell they were no deeper than the ones on my lip. It is a tribute to my parents that my positive feelings for dogs in general went unchanged. While waiting for the ambulance to take me to hospital, I evidently clung for comfort to our family dog, a matronly dachshund by the name of Linda. Some weeks later, still bruised and swollen, I was playing in our front garden when, to the horror of my mother who was watching from the bedroom window, an unknown dog stopped at the gate. Showing admirable self-control, she did not intervene as I walked towards it and reached out to stroke its head. This time the dog proved friendly, and contributed to a small victory of faith over experience.

Though I was fortunate enough to escape with only minor injuries, the other protagonists in my little drama did not fare so well. The dog was rightly 'put down' at the insistence of the police, but the old man who had come to my rescue most undeservedly died too. The effort of driving off the dog had brought on a heart attack, and he died from its effects on his way to hospital. I regret knowing nothing about him, not even his name, because I would like to be able to make some formal gesture of thanks here and salute the bravery of someone who, after all, gave his life for mine.

As a child my attitude was somewhat different: I came to relish my role as the victim of these bloodthirsty events, and the fact that my saviour had sacrificed his life on my behalf only made the story more enthralling. Later, when I became practised in the telling of my gruesome tale, it was the compulsory execution of the dog rather than the old man's death that most stirred my schoolboy audiences and convinced them they were hearing a legend of truly epic consequence.

Whatever effect it had on me, mentally and physically, my accident undoubtedly ensured that I did not grow to be the regular-featured lad who seems to be promised by the photograph in my parents' bedroom. Instead, I became lop-sided and crooked-faced, and although I did not brood on it much, this sudden, arbitrary change in my appearance helped to set in motion the suspicion, which later hardened into a morbid conviction, that I was not who I was meant to be, that my true identity was other than the warped one imposed on me. In part, this was no more than a vainglorious fantasy of the kind in which most imaginative adolescents indulge, but it was also fuelled by a feeling which is probably less common and which has dogged me, to coin a phrase, with greater or lesser ferocity for as long as I can remember – the feeling that my identity is amorphous or inadequately formed. I have been haunted by the sense that I am more mutable than is safe, that I am not only dangerously changeable, but indefinitely defined in the first place. During periods of crisis, when I came to look for my essential self, I seemed to discover only a vaporous space which bore my name yet lacked any core or consistency, and much of my life has been spent trying to give this cloud some hard and durable edges, as well as a solid centre. While never quite knowing who I am, I have always wanted to be someone else – though without knowing who that should be either.

ONE

Because it takes place before the dawn of memory, one's birth is bound to be a myth, and few stories hold more fascination for children than the book of their own genesis. When small, my children found it impossible to conceive of a world which did not contain them. In their understanding, time began only with their birth, and everything that had gone before was merely a shadow and an echo of what was to be. In order to assert her non-absence during events that had occurred long before her birth, my daughter Tilly ingeniously invented a kind of retrospective immortality for herself: she described this period, the period B.T., as it were, as the time when she was 'in mummy's tummy', an epoch that could be conveniently stretched back any number of years, often to a point well before my wife Sally and I met, and even before Sally herself was born.

As a child, I too was enthralled by the circumstances of my birth, which seemed to me wonderfully colourful and adventurous. For a start, I was delivered not in a hospital, but at home in a proper bed; a bed, moreover, which I often looked at, trying to reconstruct this first of all experiences. And I was born not in an ordinary house, but in a farm-house, for my mother was living at the time with her parents on their farm in South Wales. Although I was hardly born in a lowly cattle shed with a manger for my bed, I always tried to infuse a flavour of Bethlehem into my nativity. To the suburban children with whom I later grew up, the rural ordinariness of my story did seem exotic indeed, for most of them had never seen the hospital, far less the bed, in which they first drew breath.

When war was declared in 1939, my father, already in the Territorials, was called up, whereupon he proposed to my mother, who accepted him. The first months of their marriage were itinerant, for he was posted to camp after camp and my mother followed him, setting up temporary homes in billets all over England. In 1940, after many false starts, he was finally dispatched abroad to serve in West Africa. My mother, meanwhile, returned to her parents' home in the Pembrokeshire village of Stackpole, where my grandfather had recently become the tenant of Home Farm, a holding owned by Lord Cawdor which incorporated some of the most beautiful and dramatic coast in all Britain. She became the manageress of a canteen catering for the soldiers and airmen based at Milford Haven, and waited for my father to return. This he did in 1943, when he was invalided out of the Army, and they were able finally to make a start at leading an ordinary married life.

During her pregnancy, my mother continued to stay in Stackpole while my father studied to complete his final law exams. He joined her just before the predicted date of her labour, and they waited with ambivalent impatience for his results and my arrival. In the event, he became a father before becoming a solicitor, even though I was a fortnight late, a lapse in punctuality I have seldom been guilty of since. In that part of the country, October is notorious for its equinoctial gales which blow off the sea, lashing the long beaches and gaunt cliffs and besieging the villages along the coast with wind and water. Despite fears that the house might be cut off by flooding, deprived of electricity and telephone or made to suffer some other catastrophe that would render it inaccessible to doctor and midwife, my mother was not to be moved in her insistence on having the baby at home. And so, at my grandmother's instruction, oil lamps were filled and trimmed, the family car was tuned up and held in constant readiness with a full tank, and half a dozen milk churns were charged each day with fresh water.

The rains fell, the winds blew and the worst tides of the year boomed and foamed in the bay below the house, but having kept the household in a state of unfulfilled emergency for a fortnight my foetal self finally chose to emerge on a night when the midwife was able to cycle with ease from Stackpole village. At dawn on the morning of 23 October the doctor, who had arrived in the early hours, took a pair of forceps to my doughy skull and hauled me into the air and life. My father was woken to be told that he had a son and that his wife was tired but otherwise unscathed. As births go, mine could not have been less problematic, but in my mother's eyes, and later in my own, the little touches of rustic melodrama and the natural portents that accompanied it gave the event an almost mythical status.

Still reeling from her ordeal, my mother announced, entirely on her own initiative that the new addition was to be called James Fraser Harrison, thus making me the namesake of my other grandfather. The grandfather in whose house I had just been born, and to whom she confided this brainwave as he dandled me, his first grandson, for the first time, was understandably affronted. My relationship with him never flourished, though this can hardly be blamed on my mother's lapse of tact.

Once born I became the object of much devoted affection, which was lavished on me by the many women then living and working at the Home Farm. There was my mother, of course, my grandmother, my mother's old nanny Gladwys, and the small staff of maids who cooked and cleaned and did mysterious things with bowls and buckets in the dairy at the back of the house. My father, meanwhile, returned to Liverpool and to the firm of solicitors where he had served his articles before the war. He was offered a partnership, at a price, and there he practised for the rest of his working life, retiring in 1983 as senior partner. He also found and bought a house which was to be our home throughout my childhood and student years, and thither he took us in 1945, when I was in my ninth month.

It was thought necessary to hire a nanny to attend to me while my mother was preoccupied with the business of setting up, six years after her wedding, the first house of her married life. However, the employment of a servant at so early a stage in my father's career should not be taken to imply either precocious success on his part or a house of any grandeur. On the contrary, these first years in Liverpool are recalled by my mother as an era of grinding hardship when national austerity was rendered still harsher by the tightfistedness of my father's employers. As evidence of their penury, she will cite the fact that they could afford to drink nothing but South African sherry – a desperate plight indeed. Such perceptions are always relative, and it seems that she found it painful, even humiliating, to adapt to the confinements of my father's then small salary, which provided for a standard of living that was certainly spartan when compared with her own father's.

Our new house, 69 Aigburth Hall Avenue, was modest, three-bedroomed and detached; it had been built not long before the war, and my parents were only its second owners. The Hall, in whose honour our avenue and a few other adjacent streets were named, had long since been demolished, and I never learnt where it used to stand. To one side of us, occupying a spacious garden, was a substantial, cream-coloured Italianate villa, whose grounds had probably been foreshortened at some point to accommodate our house and its identical twin next door. For a while I used to think this was Aigburth Hall, and in its day it must have housed a wealthy family, though by our time it was serving as an orphanage. My mother occasionally sent me there to deliver in person a donation of my discarded toys. I was always greeted at the door with solemn politeness by the matron, who accepted my broken-down gifts as if they were the boon of a great philanthropist and sent me down the steps glowing with a sense of my own saintliness. I was intrigued by the inmates of this place, the recipients of my charity, but I never met one face to face. Occasionally, I saw little groups of them playing innocently, almost humbly, in the garden near the house. They must have been remarkably well behaved, or sternly disciplined, because they never climbed the sandstone wall which backed on to our garden to peer, as I often did, at their neighbours.

Not long after he bought our house, my father bought a patch of ground immediately behind it and extended our garden into the biggest in the street. In those days he was a keen and energetic gardener, spending his summer evenings and most weekends bent sweating over a fork or posed, horizontal and red-faced, behind his unyielding manual lawn mower. I used to marvel at the thick sludge of raw soil he left around the sides of our kitchen sink whenever he washed his hands after working outside. As a child I had a very small appetite, which was to become a contentious failing, and I developed a positive distaste for vegetables. It was therefore left to my parents to consume between them the prodigious output of potatoes, sprouts, cauliflowers and carrots that sprang from my father's model vegetable patch. Since they were modest eaters too and seldom entertained, I can only imagine that the bulk of his hard-won crop was either thrown away or put on his many compost heaps where it rotted richly until ready to stimulate new, still more bounteous harvests. My parents' present garden, though a picture, is quite devoid of vegetables.

My father's fecund kitchen garden was divided from the lawn by a narrow path made of compressed cinders, which he raked out of our kitchen boiler every morning, powdering his office suit with fine pink and grey dust. A second path, running at right angles, subdivided his lushly mulched vegetable plots and led to his battery of compost bins. Across this path he erected a swing for me, a huge, gaunt gallows-like affair with two tall wooden posts sunk in concrete and a narrow cross-bar. Suspended to a pair of hooks curled like rams' horns was a pair of long ropes supporting the swing seat, which as I grew bigger had to be raised each year. I passed countless hours sitting or standing on this swing, whose versatility was limitless. Without any additional props it filled the role of cowboy-horse, stage-coach, covered wagon, knight's charger, pirate ship – complete with rigging and crow's nest – jungle liana – as used by Tarzan – or acrobat's trapeze. Owing to their exceptional length, it was possible to twist the ropes until they formed a taut, springy corkscrew which, when released, would unwind at an impressive speed, inducing a mild state of hallucination in the swinger. Once, while in pursuit of this dizzy oblivion, I became entangled in the ropes and found myself hanging upside-down with no chance of escape, my life rapidly ebbing away, or so it seemed. But then I thought, 'I'm not going to die. I can't die, because children don't.' This comforting delusion calmed me instantly, and I extricated myself with ease.

As often as not, I neither played, nor actively swung, nor revolved, but simply hung like the dead weight of a pendulum, mindlessly oscillating, my whole being emptied into the dwindling arc described by my inert mass. I must have passed many hours of my early childhood in this vacant condition, and although the fact that I was an only child allowed me more time than most to indulge it, I don't think the habit was a result of my solitary state. I have noticed my own children descending into the same trance, the pleasure of which perhaps derives from reproducing our blind, softly bobbing suspension in the womb. Or perhaps it is just a way of blocking out the difficult world for a safe minute or two.

On another occasion my swing really did perform as an instrument of execution, though it was applied most unintentionally. I had been given a tortoise, a mysterious beast which trundled its way round the garden all summer, retiring on sharp nights to the fervid, sweet-smelling luxury of the tomato plants in the greenhouse. I was fond of it and wanted to share my pleasures with it, and so one afternoon I placed it on the swing and gently rocked it to and fro. As soon as the motion began, it withdrew its head and legs and lay wobbling on the seat like a stone. When at last I stopped, it poked out its head and vomited up some greenish liquid, leaving its neck drooping slackly over the edge of the seat. I put it down on the grass where it lay without moving. The next time I looked, it was dead.

The house, on the other hand, was my mother's domain, and during the twenty-two years she and my father lived there (many more years than she wanted) she utterly changed its interior. As it happened, the exterior was rather stylish, for the façade – if that is not too grand a word for the front of so humble a house – was ornamented in the art deco style with variegated bricks, coloured leaded lights and a modish little portico. She touched none of this, but as my father's income increased, as relatives died and their furniture was inherited, and, finally, as she herself began to earn surprisingly large amounts of money from the dress shop she opened, she gradually turned the inside of our three-bedroomed suburban villa into a miniature stately home. Visitors were always stunned by the grandeur to be found within its unassuming shell.

As is often the way with children, I was oblivious to these refurbishments except when they affected me directly. In the eyes of small children houses are more a matter of anthropology than aesthetics: each room seems to have its own laws and rituals, as well as its own climate, seasons and topography. For example, the lounge (so-called to distinguish it from the more informal sitting-room, and later transmuted into a dining-room) was not much used when I was a small child, at least not for functions I attended. I may perhaps have been banned from entering it, but whenever I did go in, illicitly or otherwise, I was always chilled by its atmosphere and cowed by its forbidding, mahogany twilight. My parents' bedroom, on the other hand, always seemed radiant, and although it too was furnished largely in mahogany, its polished brown surfaces gleamed and shone with a scintillating freshness. Most mornings I would run from my own hot bed along the landing and into my mother's bed, being careful to avoid the tang of early-morning tea on her breath. Otherwise, this was not a room I visited often, for its chests of drawers and skyscraper cupboards only contained my mother's clothes and shoes. On the other hand, it was the site of a most notorious crime of mine, and so perhaps it held a greater attraction than I recall.

My own children regularly ask me to tell them stories about my being naughty as a boy, but to my embarrassment the store of these is very scant. By and large I was an obedient, tractable child, to whom even mild impertinence in other children was shocking, and the notion of active rebellion inconceivable.

And yet, on this one occasion, I did perform a deed of spectacular mischief, though its enormity was not intended or foreseen. I was left in the charge of a baby-sitter, and taking advantage of her negligence I left my room, where I was assumed to be playing quietly, and stole into my parents' room. I began to play with their gas fire, and when I had removed all its clay elements, I proceeded carefully to pour water down each gas hole from the kettle my mother used to make her tea.

To anyone interested in causing a major urban disruption with the minimum of means, I can recommend this ploy. No immediate effect showed itself, but later, after my parents had found the displaced elements and telephoned the Gas Board, a virtual state of emergency was declared. Every household in the street was instructed to turn off its gas for fear of explosions, and an army of men was deployed to dig up the pavement on both sides of the road to trace how far my little trickle of water had penetrated the system. It was many hours before the neighbourhood was allowed to cook and warm itself again.

Next to my parents' bedroom and overlooking the front door was a small spare room, which would only accommodate a narrow single bed and was seldom used. Its door was generally kept shut – mostly for the sake of warmth, because the house was not centrally heated – and this closed door, standing at the top of the stairs, became one of those sites of black magic which are imperceptible to adults, but fill a child's mind with terror. The door and the patch of carpet in front of it made up a shadowy corner of the landing, by no means lightless, and during the day I crossed it without a care. But at night, when I was obliged to go upstairs on my own, I could not bring myself to put my feet in the dreaded black hole that seemed to open up before me as I approached the topmost step. I devised a way of clutching the bannisters and swinging myself over the yawning gap, and I was convinced I would only escape with my life if I carried out to the letter a complicated ritual involving certain words and movements. I had to jump off my left foot and land on my right; I had to utter a talismanic spell at just the right volume, loud enough for the bogeymen to hear, but not so loud as to alert my parents downstairs; and, most important, I had to avoid looking at the door itself. A single glance would have been enough to provoke the monsters that lurked behind it, and then I would have been finished. I could never have described the forces that lay in wait for me at the top of the stairs; all I knew was that they were sleeplessly malevolent. I did not dare tell my parents about them because they were far more powerful even than my father at his angriest, and they would exact a still more terrible revenge for my betrayal. My only hope lay in moving very fast and disarming them with my counter-sorcery; this I managed to do each time, but it was always a close-run thing.

I do not know where these fears sprang from or whose face lurked behind the bogey mask. I was a timorous child, and imaginative, but not neurotically so, and the spooks that haunted me were mostly confined to that one spot of the house. Such horrors are of course a commonplace of childhood, though no less terrifying for that. My son, now aged eight, is convinced that as soon as the sun goes down our house becomes infested with murderers whose sole ambition is to 'get' him, and no amount of looking under the bed, turning on of lights or shouting at the intruders to go away if they know what's good for them will reassure him. I suspect these irrational fears are in part a legacy of infanthood, when the world was full of inexplicable, unexpected forces which attacked and overwhelmed one, and went away just as mysteriously. Yet this capacity for embracing contradictions – Jack knows there are no murderers, but sees them stalking in every shadow – is surely a condition not so much of childhood as of being human. It is our powers of unreason, rather than those of reason, that make us a truly singular species. How else would we be able to believe in gods who never manifest themselves, in ideals which are never realized in experience, in the perfectibility of love which all relationships discredit?

Despite its compactness and minimal number of rooms, our house contained several other corners which breathed a faintly supernatural air. The hall, for example, possessed a magical aura created by the patterns of coloured glass set in the front door and the two small windows on either side. On a sunny day these cast streaks of kaleidoscopic colour across the walls and carpet, giving visitors to our atheist household an incongruous sense of entering a place of worship. At night the hall was transformed from the holy to the exotic, for it was lit by an obese and beaming Buddha made of smoked glass, whose belly concealed a bulb within its rotund folds and emanated a soft, amber glow.

In those days my father kept a large collection of swords and knives, turning our innocuous hallway into a positive armoury, and adding still more to its bizarre atmosphere. This was a curious feature of his character, because although he had not made a natural soldier during the war, and had indeed loathed his time in the Army, he took away from his unhappy experience a passion for the trappings of war – for martial music, uniforms, parades, and swords. Arranged in patterns around the walls, as if to terrify the visitor into submission before he had even entered the house, was a motley gathering of weapons, some ceremonial, some unmistakably lethal. An absurdly long dress sword, which was perhaps designed for a cavalry officer, was placed in a position of honour where its moth-eaten gold braid could be seen to advantage. I think I was forbidden to touch the sword display, but when the opportunity arose I would covertly take down this Excalibur and sneak it out of its crumbling leather scabbard to test the sharpness of its blade. Not realizing that its function was entirely cosmetic, I was always disappointed to find that its wicked-looking length of steel was quite blunt from end to end. More rewarding was a pair of curved Nepalese *kukris*, for they not only looked, but also felt wonderfully bloodthirsty. Like some species of marsupial, they carried baby replicas of themselves in little pouches at the front of their scabbards, and these too were murderously sharp.

In spite of its name, the sitting-room was where we ate most of our meals, and these took place at an oak gate-leg table which was supported by what seemed to be a small forest of black poles growing out of the carpet. The food was served from the kitchen through a hatch, which my mother would whisk open like a magician. The furniture in the room always appeared huge to me, but this was probably not the result of a childish distortion, because much of it had been inherited from more spacious houses. My parents sat in a pair of massive armchairs made of cow-hide which had dark-brown velvet cushions to match the shade of the leather. Years of polishing had given their sides and arms the lustre of mahogany, which was in keeping with most of my parents' other legacies. They were monsters, I suppose, and would have done justice to the ranch-house of a Texas cattle baron; yet they were wonderfully comfortable, and when affluence allowed my mother to discard them in favour of something more elegantly covered, my father insisted on having his new chair built to exactly the same dimensions.

I do not know how old I was when my parents abandoned their attempts to have another child, or simply despaired of it, but from my earliest days I was installed in the second large bedroom which, like theirs, ran the length of the house and had a large window at either end. One overlooked the garden and the other, a bay of six leaded lights set with lozenges of coloured glass, overlooked the street. When I was fourteen or so I was given a small leather-topped, kneehole desk, and it stood in this bay, allowing me, under the guise of studious concentration, to ogle the office girls who made their way to and from the bus stop at the end of our road. I still have the desk, though it lies discarded and unused in my son's bedroom, but to this day I use the chair I used then, an unpadded armchair with a cane disc for a back. I also have in my present bedroom the mahogany chest of drawers where my toys and clothes were kept, and standing beside me now is the bookcase which housed the books I bought when bibliomania first gripped me. I find the sense of continuity embodied in these pieces of furniture profoundly consoling, and by the same token I keenly regret the loss of other pieces which I might have kept, but let go through carelessness or the need for ready cash. I am forty-two years old, and although my way of life over the last decade or so has been settled I will have to stay in this house, using this room as my study, for many more years before I clock up the same number of hours as I passed in that room, which was successively my nursery, bedroom and study and finally the spare room where my first wife and I slept when we paid visits to my parents.

Had I not been an only child, I would not be placing such stress on the significance of a mere room, but because I was not just an only child, but also a bookish and introspective child whose friends were mostly made far away from home at boarding school, this room was the metropolis of my small world, from which I seldom strayed during the holidays. It became both an enclosing shell and the outer case of my very skull. As I grew older it evolved from being the indoor field on which my knights fought their jousting tournaments and my Dinky trucks made their endless, fruitless journeys of exploration, and turned itself into my ivory tower, my chamber at 221B Baker Street, my wizard's den, my laboratory where I cooked up those ideas which my mother found increasingly unintelligible and my father found increasingly repugnant. Here I read, wrote, dreamed and simply lolled about with that inexhaustible listlessness that is so maddening to parents and so essential to the sanity of adolescents. Here too, on the bed where I had slept for nineteen years in solitude, if not innocence, I attempted my first seduction.

In spite of my terror of the landing outside my room, I perversely insisted on sleeping in the dark, without a night-light, and to this day I can only get to sleep in tomb-like conditions of darkness and silence. As a small child, sent to bed while the rest of the world was still on the move, I would lie in the blackness listening out for cars on the road below and waiting for their headlamps to pierce the gap above my curtains. The coloured glass in my windows would turn the beams into rainbow graffiti sprayed for a moment across my ceiling, and then the inky velvet would drop again, unbroken by any chink or glow of light. On winter nights I would listen to the lugubrious honk of the foghorn which was stationed somewhere upstream to warn ships off the Devil's Bank and the Dungeon Banks, and I would imagine the thick, chill water of the Mersey swelling over its concrete bank, flooding the Promenade, flooding the cricket ground, and swirling up Aigburth Hall Avenue to sink our house and drown us all. Strangely enough, this fantasy was more comforting than disturbing, and by the time the insurgent waves were lapping round my father's bus stop, I was usually submerged in sleep.

TWO

My mother was the daughter of a farmer turned businessman, who in middle age reverted once more to farming. Thus, she looked both ways in her upbringing, to the city (Manchester) where her father worked, and to the country where his heart was and where she often visited the clan of aunts and uncles on her mother's side, who were Cheshire farmers. Having left Lowther College, an academy for young ladies which taught her such invaluable skills as how to peel and eat a banana using nothing but a knife and fork, she began to train and work as a mannequin, much to her father's horror. It was during this period of her parading up and down catwalks in the hotels of

Liverpool, Manchester and even London that my father met her at a dinner-dance. In 1938 her father resigned from Shell and moved his family to the Home Farm at Stackpole, cutting short my mother's career and making my father's courtship highly inconvenient. The outbreak of war intervened, however, and within three months they were married; not in Pembroke, but in West Kirby where my father's parents then lived. During their period of enforced separation, my mother cemented her attachment to her parents' new home, which in later years came to represent for her an Eden from which she had been expelled, but not without the right to return now and again.

And so, when she travelled up from Pembroke in 1945, bringing her child and dog, to say nothing of the nanny, and joined my father in the newly acquired 69 Aigburth Hall Avenue, she was embarking on a way of life for which she was not well prepared. My father himself must still have been something of a stranger to her, for although they had been married for five years they still had not lived together in their own house. She was not used to suburbia, to the drab landscape – as it must have seemed to her – of undistinguished streets, of poor shops, of row upon row of small houses concealing small, respectable lives. She was not used to being in a small house all day with nobody for company except a child. She was not used to living on slender means (although admittedly these were supplemented from various sources). She was not used to Liverpool; to its squalor, its poverty and its violence. She was not used to living amidst ruins, for this was the Liverpool razed by the German bombers (soon to be razed still more devastatingly by municipal planners); and finally, she was not used to being submerged in the catarrhal smog which in those days lay over the city like a shroud. For all these reasons the earliest years of her marriage proper were not the happiest of my mother's life. She had to make enormous adjustments, something to which she was not temperamentally prone (any more than I am now), and most of the changes she underwent she found either humiliating or unwelcome. She had to re-invent herself as a wife, a mother, and a woman, and being a perfectionist she was not easily reconciled to the results, which were bound to be more makeshift than ideal.

I, of course, had no inkling of any of this. As far as small children are concerned, normality is what is – the immediate given – no matter how unstable or inappropriate it may seem to their parents. Children have no history by which to measure disappointment against expectation. But my mother did not vent her unhappiness on me; on the contrary, I became her chief source of consolation. Naturally I had no idea that I was enjoying an extraordinary relationship, but by the standards of everyday intercourse, and even by the standards of mother-child relations, ours was extraordinary. After all, I was never again in my life to receive one woman's exclusive attention and affection throughout my every waking hour. Yet that was our situation during those first days in Liverpool: my father was away on his daily crusade to the office, I had no sibling to compete with, and there were no other members of our household to divert my mother. At that stage, she did not own a car and had no local friends. For her part, this continual exposure to one other person must have been a strange experience. As a child she had always had her brother with whom to share her parents' affection, and in any case her mother had worked as a teacher during her early childhood, leaving her in the care of a nanny, Gladwys, whom I remember as a wizened old woman with a lightly bristled chin. To be confined to the company of a single person, a child further-more, within a small, otherwise empty house, surrounded by virtual strangers in a strange town, was therefore as new to her as it seemed normal to me.

When I look back on my early childhood, I find it difficult to reconstruct my parents as they were then. They were an enveloping medium, the portable environment of my being, but they have retained no sharpness of outline as personalities or even as images. Like most parents, they were the oxygen of my childhood, in which I flourished, and as such they were so ubiquitous that they have become invisible to memory. Children, in any case, are uninterested in the complexities of adult character, and largely oblivious to their parents' traits unless these obtrude unavoidably, in which case they are usually a source of embarrassment and distress. For instance, my mother has always been strikingly chic in her choice of clothes, but this obvious fact quite escaped my attention until, when I was fourteen or so, the local paper nominated her the city's 'best-dressed woman', publishing a photograph of her in full regalia in Bold Street. This aspect of my mother came home to me as a revelation and a shock, though it also made me proud. My father, presumably by virtue of being absent for most of my short day and thus the object of special observation when he was at home, swims through the murk of recall in slightly brighter colours than my mother. But my childhood feelings for my mother, so far as I recall them, were strong and serene. I knew I was loved, and of course I loved her in return. My memories of those earliest days are unmingled with any sense of unease, and I have my mother to thank for this bedrock of security.

I may be doing her an unjustice, but I do not think she played with me much; on the other hand, I probably did not often ask her, for I was always content to amuse myself, a capacity which was no doubt refined by my being an only child. She did, however, take me on modest expeditions, and I enjoyed these with the keenest relish. Our ritual of walking up the road to the row of shops on Booker Avenue not only gave me a lifelong taste for shopping, but has left me feeling that a day without seeing the inside of a shop is incomplete. For longer trips we would resort to my mother's bicycle, a cumbersome black Raleigh of sit-up-and-beg design equipped with a child's seat over the rear mudguard. We must have made a comical sight, for as I grew older and less infatuated with the sheer pleasure of motion, I took to reading on our journeys, lolling idly while my mother toiled and panted in front of me.

In summer these heroic efforts would usually take us to Sefton Park, still one of the finest municipal parks in the country, where we would walk round the Serpentine and admire the home-made speedboats as they dashed across the water in creaming arcs, quite disregarded by the ornamental ducks hanging around the bank in the hope of food. There were swans, too, which used to nest in a secluded spot on a little island until one year a gang of boys stoned and killed them as they sat on their eggs. I remember my mother's shock and disgust when my father came home with this story; it became her symbol for Liverpool's perverted brutality.

Leaving the lake, we would make our way through landscaped hillocks and past sandstone grottoes, where kids did unspeakable things to each other on Saturday afternoons, towards the Palm House, which I thought – and still think – is a magical place. From the outside it looks like a crystal balloon hovering over the dusty corporation grass, and inside it makes you feel you are exploring a jungle trapped in a huge swimming bubble. In the hot, sweet atmosphere, its elegant ironwork pillars, spiral staircases and coiling galleries seem to grow as luxuriantly as the trees and creepers themselves. Warm from our tropical excursion, we could come outside to choose a bench in the sun and eat our lunch, overlooked by a statue of Darwin, Newton or some other scientific worthy condemned for his achievements to be streaked with guano.

For a couple of weeks during each summer holidays Bertram Mills' Circus used to set up camp on the other side of the park and my mother would take me, every day if possible, to visit the animals in their cages, which formed a sort of impromptu zoo behind the Big Top. With its deliciously fetid smell of dung and somnolent animals, this too was a magical spot. Encouraged by a hospitable keeper who allowed me to help him feed the elephants, I formed an ambition to work with animals myself, which persisted in a variety of forms well into adolescence. Unfortunately our friend the keeper, mistaking our interest in his animals for an interest in him, became a little too hospitable and made a pass at my mother (as I discovered many years later), and so, much to my uncomprehending annoyance, our visits had to be abruptly discontinued.

On fine days in winter, or when we only wanted a short outing, we could cross the main road which took my father to and from his office and walk from the palatial Aigburth Cricket Club down Riversdale Road towards the Mersey. As luck would have it, the stretch of bank nearest to us was the first to be developed in what is now the completed Otterspool Promenade, which reaches two miles downstream to the Dingle and was the site of the Garden Festival in 1984. Amidst all the chaos, ugliness and stupidity of Liverpool's post-war building, 'the Prom' stood out as a wonderful exception, for it was both well designed and properly maintained. At all events, my mother and I often went there to eat our lunch and exercise the dogs. Later I used to go on my own, mostly to roller-skate, for its sinuous network of sloping paths and noble esplanade were perfectly adapted to skating. And later still, as a mooning adolescent, I took myself there almost every day to commune with the water, which served for me, and many others, as a muddy balm.

An inevitable part of these highly ritualized visits was to stand at the railings, gazing across the swirling brown surface of the river towards Port Sunlight (as grotesque a misnomer as the Dingle), and with great deliberation to breathe in the air. This was more of a liquid than a gas, and possessed a singular odour – a pungent and unforgettable mix of sterile mud, salt and effluent. Up and down the entire length of the boulevard people could be observed earnestly heaving in huge lungfuls of the stuff in the belief that it was in some way salubrious. That can hardly have been the case, since in those days the Mersey was the most badly polluted river in Britain and its majestic waters were utterly lifeless. Yet there was no question that, whatever poisons it contained, the breeze that always blew so briskly off its waves was strangely intoxicating.

Although I certainly did not realize it at the time, these trips to the river and the park were a vital part of my mother's search for a vestige of the countryside within the brick and metal wasteland of her new home, a patch of green where the air seemed cleaner and where the horizon did not crowd the eye. Liverpool possesses many such corners and my mother had a good nose for discovering them. If she infused our outings with a little melancholy, none of it soaked into me, for I learnt to love the eccentric beauty of the places she found, and I am still irresistibly drawn to them whenever I find myself in Liverpool.

The somewhat black picture I have painted of my mother's first years in Aigburth must be mitigated by the appearance of the friends she began to make, notably the Franklands, a couple who lived literally round the corner and who also had an only child, a girl exotically named Leonore. The four adults enjoyed a casual intimacy which was unique in my parents' experience. After the Franklands moved to London some years later they never found another couple to whom they could open their door with the same ease and affability. Leonore's mother treated me with an air of flirtatious amusement and her voice chuckled with tobacco huskiness; on both these counts I thought her most glamorous. Likewise, Leonore's father cut an impressive figure in my eyes: he drove a sports car, wore a highly mobile moustache which he would preen in a swash-buckling gesture made with the back of his hand, and adopted a 'silly-ass' voice when talking to Leonore and me. However, these splendid characteristics apart, Leonore's parents scarce-ly existed as fully-fledged people to me; they were simply, as I am to my children's friends, part of the material environment, members of the staff who served us, and occasionally harried us, and whom we mostly took for granted.

With Leonore herself I had a sunny, entirely harmonious relationship of the sort perhaps only young children can achieve. We spent whole days together, day after day, and I have no memory of any antagonism between us. We were absorbed in a state of deep playfulness, requiring nothing of each other which we could not give, and giving nothing that was resented. It is often said that only children develop inflated egos, having suffered no competition in the nursery, and that this may lead to an incapacity for friendship. But in my experience the opposite is the truth, and only children have, if anything, a special gift for making close friendships. Since we have no siblings to befriend, we are driven by simple necessity to socialize outside the nursery, and the very fact that we place an unusually high value on ourselves enables us, paradoxically, to extend a certain amicable tolerance to others.

Not all my relationships with other children, even other only children, were as harmonious as the one with Leonore. For instance, my parents were friendly with a couple whose marriage had been blessed with a son called Timothy, a mischievous lad referred to by my mother as 'a bit of a handful'. Whenever he and his mother came for tea, fortunately a rare occurrence, we boys would be bundled off to my room under severe instructions (his mother had a ferocious temper) to play quietly. Timothy's method of play was to remove all the drawers of my toy cupboard and shake out their contents, not playing with anything but reducing the room to ruins. I would watch in helpless horror, for my mother had very strict rules about tidying up at the end of the day and his ransacking condemned me to hours of work. When I was taken to play at his house, more often than not dressed in my scarlet waistcoat, he would fight me; or rather he would try, for I never retaliated. I just accepted his punches with a sort of wet defiance until he grew bored and stopped. I complained about this to my mother, who advised me to stand up for myself and hit him back if he tried to start another fight. The next time we called for tea, mother and son stood at their garden gate, greeting us with smiles and waves, but I leapt from the car, and before Timothy had uttered a word, far less challenged me, I smote him violently in the face. Thereafter, the two mothers met during school hours, and my 'friendship' with Timothy was considered extinct.

As well as Leonore, I had two other friends who lived within walking distance. Tony Mason, now a bearded and grizzled journalist and a father himself, must be counted my oldest friend, since we first met, if that is the word, while being wheeled in parallel prams on the way to the shops on Booker Avenue. After many moves and vicissitudes, Tony now lives in the same part of Cheshire as my parents and we regularly see each other. Brian Bramson, my other friend, I have not seen for many years and probably would not recognize, though I vividly recall his five-year-old self, a black-haired, curly-headed, capering imp of a boy who was always in high spirits and always curious. The three of us, together with Leonore, formed a casual gang and circulated from house to house, mostly in order to play cowboys and Indians. I identified closely with Hopalong Cassidy, he of the white hair and black outfit, and I adopted his name for the purposes of our shoot-outs. Leonore allowed herself to be known as Cactus Kate, but she did not carry a gun, unlike the rest of us who were invariably armed to the teeth. Wearing our hats, scarves, belts and holsters, we galloped everywhere, slapping our buttocks and clicking our teeth, and when we stopped to shoot the baddies we never shot more than six rounds without reloading; nor did we forget to make the appropriate ricochet noise – peeowaaaang – as our bullets bounced off the rocks. Sometimes the chase would end in our capturing Leonore, temporarily demoted to a squaw, who would be roped to the laburnum tree while we rode round her, whooping and firing. She would indulge us for a while, letting us have our fun, but when her patience ran out she would simply untie herself and, without any rancour or sign of dislike, walk herself home.

For all the children in our gang, life in those days was suburban, conventional and, I would guess, reasonably happy; it certainly was for me. That period is symbolized in my mind by what a psychoanalyst would call a screen memory – a kind of private folk myth which though trivial in itself represents a whole passage of experience. It is not even an incident; merely a scene. A sunny Sunday morning in summer. My father has taken me with him on some errand to a part of our neighbourhood which is near our house, yet unfamiliar to me. I hold his hand, and as we walk along the pavement we look over walls and fences and hedges at people mowing their lawns, digging their flowerbeds, washing their windows, hosing their cars, and reading their papers in deck-chairs. From every house comes the noise of the Billy Cotton Band Show and the aroma of roast beef. My father cracks jokes with strangers, who laugh at them. There is no traffic on the street except for boys idling on their bikes, and the only other people on the pavement are children kicking balls or playing hop-scotch. In short, it is a picture of suburbia at ease with itself, contentedly going about its Sunday business.

I associate two connected emotions with this memory, both of an intensity quite out of proportion to its sentimental tone. First, I remember an almost ecstatic sense of pleasure arising from the sheer thrill of walking beside my father, holding his hand, being with him on his own and having him talk to me. Second, I remember my feeling of pride as down those mild streets he went, strolling so confidently, so benevolently through an Aigburth which might have been a little state ruled by him and men like him. And it was an Aigburth he would bequeath to me, his heir.

At the heart of my parents' philosophy was a belief in

normality, a state of affairs in which everything ran smoothly and everyone behaved appropriately. After the monstrous abnormality of the war, their generation can hardly be blamed for craving an orderly ordinariness in their civil life. For my mother this was more of an ideal than a reality, since the world she inhabited tended to fall very short of normal most of the time by being too dirty, too inconvenient and perhaps too dull. My father, for his part, has become increasingly despondent in his view of Britain and what he sees as its decline into idleness and indiscipline, a Britain that will never return to the lost standards of the 'thirties. But in the days of my childhood, the world, or at any rate his patch of it, did more or less conform to my father's expectations, and it was his genial delight in all he saw about him that I sensed on our Sunday stroll. I was thrilled to be his lieutenant on this tour of inspection and to be sharing in his contentment.

In due course my horizons, and those of Leonore, Anthony and Brian, were pushed a mile or so beyond Aigburth, for when we were six we were all sent to school a bus-ride away.

I had already had a taste of education, having been bicycled by my mother for two or three mornings a week to the house of a large family which employed a governess but needed to defray the cost by recruiting extra children to the class. There were seven or eight of us, mostly girls, and we gathered in a large front room with a bay window which acted as a sort of throne for the governess, Miss Yates. Throughout our lessons she never stood up, but sat square and upright, with her long skirts entirely hiding her chair and giving her the look of a monumental tea cosy. She wore her white hair in a bun and her stern face was softened by a chin that loosened into a heap of little folds on her collar as if it were melting. She had an air of tremendous authority, or so I thought, though it did nothing to cow the youngest member of the host family. He was officially too young to attend our classes, which would always start without him, but sooner or later he would manage to infiltrate them, whereupon he would run round the room yelling and flinging books on the floor until he was captured and ejected. His naughtiness shocked me, for when his mother told him to stop and threatened to punish him, he simply laughed at her, and I had never seen a child do that. I had certainly never behaved that way myself; indeed, it had never occurred to me that such an option was available.

I must have been taught to read and write by Miss Yates, though I have no memory of *learning* to do either; reading came especially easily to me. I did, however, struggle over French, which we were made to speak during mock tea parties, passing each other '*un morceau de gâteau*', '*du beurre, s'il vous plaît* ', and so on. I was taught the language for the next fourteen years, but never got my tongue round it. I probably spoke it with more facility under Miss Yates's quaint regime that I have done ever since.

At my primary school, life was pleasant and stimulating. Like most other pupils there I thrived, which is no doubt the reason why it has left so little trace on my memory. A couple of incidents remain, but no more. During my first term I was encircled one morning on the playground by a ring of boys.

'You're a yid,' said one.

I had no idea what he meant.

'You're a Jew-boy.'

'No, I'm not,' I said, indignantly. I had heard people referred to as 'Jews', and indeed my parents had the inevitable friend who was Jewish, a fact they often commented on, but beyond knowing that I was not a Jew I did not know what they were.

'He must be a Jew. Look at his nose.'

The ring closed menacingly round me as I protested more and more shrilly.

'Then you must be a Catholic,' said the boy, determined to find some reason for hitting me.

'I'm not a Catholic. Honest.' I begged.

'What are you?'

'I was born in Little England Beyond Wales,' I declared, courage suddenly coming to my aid. 'On a farm.'

My unexpected reply, with its mysterious appeal to patriotism, disconcerted them for a moment, and I ran for it.

This took place five or six years after the end of the war, when the fact of the Holocaust, if not its full scope, must have been known to everyone, yet in this school that was pleasantly free of every other form of bullying, anti-Semitism was common, even if it never amounted to much more than playground insults and the odd scuffle.

In other respects, those were innocent days. After I had been at the school a term or two, it was arranged that I should walk home on my own or take the bus, a journey of a mile or so, and this I did in a loitering fashion, relishing the little interlude of freedom between school and home. The trip was given the smack of adventure by the warning that a gang of boys from another school sometimes hung about Brodie Avenue, on the bus route, waiting their chance to bash up posh kids, but in the event I was never attacked or even taunted.

In the classroom I was taught by Miss Renshaw, who was motherly, and later by Miss Black, who was frightening by virtue of her curved and pointed chin, which resembled a huge thorn, but who was also a forceful teacher. The Stones, who owned the school, took a special interest in me, telling my parents they thought I was 'scholarship material', a phrase I knew to be a compliment, though at first I could not understand its naval implications. What was this ship? I did not really believe my alleged cleverness meant I would be sent away to sea, but I was puzzled nevertheless and far too proud to admit my ignorance by asking.

The Stones occasionally invited me to tea at their home, an airless bungalow whose small rooms were tainted with the odour of cats. I always felt uncomfortable there, not only because of the feline mustiness in the air, but because I could not reconcile the superhuman figures of the headmaster and his wife, who strode like giants around the school's airy enormity, with this pottering old couple in their box of a house. Their complete deficiency as civilians was confirmed in my mind one summer evening when they took me for a walk in Calderstones Park. Reaching a secluded spot in a little glade, they looked furtively around, then pulled a pair of trowels out of a bag and proceeded to stuff it with leaf mould. They dug, on their knees, with the frantic desperation of the truly guilty, while at the same time explaining to me in their teachers' voices the invaluable properties of the black muck they were exhuming. I stared down at them in a mixture of disbelief and repulsion, and was greatly relieved when at last they stood up. They were in fact kindly people, if a little eccentric, who had taken me under their wing, but the judgement of childhood can be very cold, especially when a priggish nerve is touched.

Mr Stone taught Latin to a small group of boys, including myself, who were due to leave his school in mid-career for boarding preparatory schools. I never discussed our impending fate with any of the other boys, but then there was really nothing to discuss. I had no idea of what was to come.

THREE

Every summer holiday and Christmas we went down to Stackpole to stay with my grandparents on their farm. In the early days, before my parents had a car, we did the journey by rail and it took all day, involving three changes of train and a longish drive from Llandeilo, where my grandfather collected us in his Daimler. I remember none of these first visits except the one when we brought a kitten home from the farm. It resembled a powder-puff on legs and in time grew into a huge and handsome neuter answering to the name of Alexander, with nothing in his dignified manner and plumed appearance to suggest that he was in fact a farmyard mongrel and not a

43

pedigree Persian Blue. Throughout his long life he was noted for his stately composure, a characteristic which he displayed even as a tiny kitten, for in the carriage he ignored the attentions of our two dachshunds and remained curled up on my lap for the entire journey, three changes and all.

I recall more clearly the journeys we made by car, though they have fused together into a single, representative memory. We always tried to set off early, but the day never began well because my father found the business of packing the car a terrible chore on which he vented his hatred of upheaval and his resentment at having to go to Stackpole. Out in the dark he would be discovered hurling suitcases round the garage and raging against the extravagant quantities of clothes my mother dragged round with her. I was always in trouble too, either for bringing too much 'rubbish' of my own or for not helping him enough. Whatever he did in the way of packing up the car was inevitably wrong. When he had rammed the last case into the boot, my mother would emerge to inspect his efforts.

'Oh Brian, you can't put that box under the heavy case. Everything will be creased.'

Fuming and sighing, he would shuffle the box round.

'Not there. You can see it will get damp if it rains.'

'Well, where then?' he would beg wearily.

'Use your common sense,' she would bark before she stormed off, leaving him baffled and furious.

I think the first car my parents owned was a Morris Minor given to them by my Stackpole grandfather; at all events, it was certainly a small car, and once my father had completed his explosive labours with the suitcases, the dog and I would be required to squeeze ourselves into a box-like space on the back seat no bigger than our combined widths. These were more or less equal since she was gross and I was the size of the legendary beanpole. This dog, incidentally, was the successor to the two previous incumbents, a mother and her wretchedly spoilt only daughter, who had comforted me after the attack on my nose and belonged to the era of our travelling by train. These had fallen victim to a spinal disease common among dachshunds and, following a decent interval of mourning, had been replaced by my travelling companion, Cherry. She too was a dachshund, and was a dog of exceptionally sweet temperament, but she suffered from two grave failings. She was ungovernably greedy, and though an idle dog to whom walks, and indeed any form of mobility apart from eating, were anathema, she was driven by her appetite to the most energetic and ingenious strategems in order to find food. As a puppy, she had skipped the lean and lithe stage and had grown directly into a small, black, over-stuffed globe; hence her name. Her adult shape was precisely that of a cartoonist's dachshund: it resembled an inflated condom, and the likeness did not stop there, for she was almost hairless too. Poor creature, she was attacked by an incurable skin infection which stripped her black coat off in patches and left her skin bald, cracked and leathery. She was, I suppose, repellent, perhaps even horrifying, but I never noticed it myself. I was used to her ugliness, and I adored her.

Wedged in our kennel with a rug tucked round us, Cherry and I made ourselves unobtrusive as my father finally jerked the overloaded car out of the garage and into the deserted streets, pausing at the end of our road, to my mother's wrath, and running back to the house to check for the umpteenth time that the gas had been turned off and the front door properly locked. A fraught silence would be maintained until we reached the Mersey Tunnel, which marked the boundary between everyday Liverpool and the road that led to Stackpole, and later to Portmeirion and my prep school as well. Only when we had emerged from the white, tiled intestine of the Tunnel did my parents relax and begin to talk, which never failed to fascinate me. All three of us embarked on our visits to Stackpole with mixed emotions, but at this stage, with the ordeal of packing and setting off behind us and the family conflicts to come still well ahead of us, my parents usually gave way to optimism and holiday spirits.

The journey itself, in the early days an eight-hour affair, was like all family activities dominated by its own rituals, which with each trip became more elaborate. We always stopped at the same spot on the Denbeigh moors for elevenses, which always consisted of coffee for my parents, milk for me, and lumps of 'crunchy', my mother's sticky, syrupy version of flapjacks. Somewhere to the south of Lake Bala, which we always admired for its dramatic beauty, I was always overcome by carsickness. I think I was actually sick only once, but my parents always dreaded a repetition and were very alert to my symptoms – green pallor, rolling eyes, convulsive swallowing, temples clammy with sweat and a complete inability to talk. The moment these were manifested the car was stopped and I was walked up and down the road – often the same stretch of road – which always cured me. Then I was allowed to take my mother's seat in the front for the last leg of the journey before lunch, which we always took at the same hotel in Machynlleth.

And so the journey went, the miles shortened by these cherished rites. During the afternoon my mother would sometimes take over the driving and my father would volunteer to sit in the back. This was my favourite arrangement. My father looked so comical crammed into my small hole with Cherry on his knee, there being no room for her beside him. At first she would lie like a beached seal, her eyes bulging in amazement at the view flashing in front of her, but soon enough her head would droop and she would sink back into sleep. I enjoyed my mother's style of driving, which involved a flamboyant use of hand signals and had more than a touch of the daredevil about it, seeming to carry us along far faster than my father's. After tea, one of the few optional items on our programme, my father would resume the wheel and we would begin to count off the landmarks that told us we had nearly finished our north-south crossing of Wales and were being reeled in across the last few miles to Stackpole.

We passed the castle at Carew, which in my opinion did not deserve the title because from the road it appeared to have no towers or keep, as a proper castle should. We dropped down into Pembroke, counting the little pebble-dash cottages that stood in a sloping row at the edge of the town, their roofs forming a set of steps. Wheeling past the office where my uncle had his auctioneering business and taking the road south to the sea, we looked back at the great circular keep of Pembroke Castle – a real castle, this, which lours over the town and is still, after seven hundred years, a potent symbol of the conqueror's heel on the neck of the Welsh. I imagined I could see the pointed metal helmets of the sentries glinting between the battlements. Approaching the final furlong now, we turned sharply at the bottom of Sampson's Hill, where a huge stone cowshed stood, and left the road half a mile further on to bump down the drive marked with a sign reading 'Private – Home Farm Only', words which always gave me a pleasant snobbish tingle. We drove past the lodge where Ada and her husband lived, though she would be waiting for us in the kitchen at the farm, past the paddock where a bull was tethered by a heavy metal bar and condemned to good behaviour by the company of a foul-tempered donkey, past the men stumping home from work who raised their fingers to their caps in a timeless gesture of deference which in later years made me cringe, past the bridge across the Lily Ponds, past the dairy and into the yard, where we parked at the back door and rushed into the house to find Grandma, leaving my father where he had begun, raging over the luggage and complaining that no one ever helped him.

Inside the kitchen, working at the long pine table that stood alongside the Aga and beneath the rack for drying clothes, would be my grandmother, Ada the cook, and a couple of maids, and sitting on one of the gigantic windowsills – the walls of the house were more than two feet thick – would be Gladwys, the tip of her nose and the end of her chin almost touching as she grimaced in concentration over her sewing. I would be kissed, and asked if I had been carsick, and told that I had grown, and as soon as possible I would escape out to the yard again, evading my struggling father, and run across to the cowsheds that stood opposite the house and formed part of the loose quadrangle of the yard.

First I went into the calfshed and let the calves coil their fish-scale tongues round my fingers, their eyes swelling white, their mouths frothing and their curly pates thumping against the bars as they sucked emptily at my dry hand. Wiping my slimy fingers on the straw, I went through to the main shed where the cows waiting to calve were stalled, great matrons lounging on their boudoirs, chewing their leisurely cud and quite indifferent to my antics. Little nuggets of brown cattle-cake stood in buckets outside each pen, and I loved to hurl them round the rafters and up and down the whitewashed alleys. I did this almost compulsively, standing in silent terror after each fusillade in case one of the men should catch me, and then firing another volley. The heavy beams above me were coated in white powder from meal and dust, which thickened the cobwebs hanging everywhere into heavy, pendulous chains and swags. They were also decorated with rosettes of every colour and class from shows all over the country, for my grandfather was an expert breeder of cattle. Lastly, I stood on a box to stare at the bull in his high-security pen and dart a nervous hand through the rails, rubbing his woolly forehead and pulling at his horns as my grandfather did on his daily inspection.

This trip round the cowsheds was the final stage in the ritual of our journey. I did not feel I had truly arrived until I had made my tour of these animals, who in their benign, uninterested way offered me a welcome free of the complications that awaited all of us inside the house.

I was my grandfather's only grandson, and yet in spite, or perhaps because of that, I was a disappointment, even an annoyance, to him. Had I been a girl, as my two cousins were, he might have indulged me. Had I reminded him of my mother, his beloved daughter, instead of my father, his regrettable son-in-law, he might have been more tolerant of my ineptitude around the farm. But these are adult speculations which have only occurred to me since. Children do not analyse the relationships in which they find themselves or attempt to explain the behaviour of others; they simply live with the effects and submit to them as they do to the weather, enjoying the sunshine and hiding from the rain, but not questioning the origins of either.

Short and vigorous, with a bristling moustache and an energetic smile, my grandfather was bluff and brisk in manner, direct in his speech, hearty in his humour, and gave every appearance of being a genial fellow who nevertheless knew his own mind and did not suffer fools gladly. And, by and large, reality matched appearance, although he was probably harder on his family than outsiders realized; with them he was always at his most jovial. As a child, I was always conscious of the fact that he was forceful and that my parents deferred to him, as did everyone around him, including my uncle, who helped him run the farm, and even my grandmother, who in her own way was also a strong character. While not a tyrant, my grand-father was nevertheless the absolute ruler of his household, and though his regime was for the most part benevolent, it was quite inflexible. For example, he was a teetotaller, having taken the pledge as a young man, and the house was therefore dry. He was known to take a glass of sherry at parties from time to time, but he never drank at home, never offered his guests a drink, and forbade his family to take alcohol in any form while under his roof. There was one occasion, which passed into family folklore, when a couple of businessmen, who had enjoyed the doubtful liberality of his water jug before, came to lunch and daringly decided to supply their own refreshment in the shape of a modest bottle of beer each. The contentious bottles were put out on the table by the maid, but as soon as my grandfather saw them he had them removed and informed his guests that they were welcome to drink beer providing they did so in their own car out in the yard.

This ban put my parents in a difficult position, for they were fond of a drink, especially when on holiday or in a social situation which called for extra courage – and Stackpole represented both conditions – yet they dared not challenge the house rules. As a result, they were obliged to fortify themselves in furtive secrecy from a bottle of whisky concealed in their bedroom.

My own feelings for him were confused and contradictory. As I grew older, direct contact with him became fraught with an anxiety which easily degenerated into simple fear. As is so often the case with families, meals were the times when conflict was most likely to flare up, and I was usually both the trigger and the victim of the explosion. My grandfather would heap up my plate and urge me in his hearty, mocking way to polish it all off, but having only a small appetite and finicky tastes I was never able to gratify him. Instead, I would sit glumly fiddling with the cold mess in front of me, my throat constricted with a mouthful I could neither chew nor swallow, and tears welling wretchedly from my eyes. The table would fall into a tense silence as he glowered at me and my parents mutely willed me to rally and clean my plate, or at least make a brave show of trying. I never did, and they never interceded to save me from what I now realize was his method of bullying them as much as me. I could only languish in clogged misery, waiting for relief. Sometimes he would contemptuously excuse me, telling me to ring for the maid to clear the table; sometimes my tears would become uncontrollable and my mother would take me from the room. I did not resent my parents' failure to protect me; indeed, it never occurred to me that they might do so. I instinctively understood their fear of him and their reluctance to make a scene by defying him, although these incidents cannot have improved my respect for their own authority over me.

In spite of all this, I cannot say I ever hated my grandfather. My parents never acknowledged his unkindness or discussed it with me; on the contrary, they spoke to me of 'Grandpa' as if he were the jolly old chap grandfathers are supposed to be, and it was many years before I myself recognized that there was a contradiction between my feelings for my tormentor and my other feelings for Grandpa.

Despite his sneering and teasing; despite his treating me like a fool, which made me behave like one; despite his mocking me for being a 'towny' and a 'city slicker', the sin of my father for which I was being punished; despite the sense of fear and belittlement I always felt in his presence, I was proud of him and proud to be his only grandson. I grew up knowing that he was not only frightening, but remarkable, and that the Home Farm, Stackpole, which in those days was enjoying its most expansive phase, was his remarkable achievement. I had no other farm to compare it with except a quaint little dairy farm in Aigburth, which was incongruously lodged in a back street behind a row of shops and consisted of a muck-spattered yard and a single row of ancient milking stalls, but it was not just the scale of his farm that told me my grandfather was an unusual man. I sensed, as children are very quick to do, his confidence and ambition. In later, less happy days, these qualities, which he never lost, were no longer rewarded with success, and they took on a somewhat crazy air as he overreached himself with schemes too expensive to win back his investment. But when I was a child the farm flourished, and it showed in every spry step he took, every order he barked out – never forgetting to add 'if you please' to his men – and every gesture he made with his thick, square finger as he pointed out the site of some new, pioneering venture. When asked when I was small what I wanted to be when I grew up, I used to reply 'a farmer', which was one of the few things about me that pleased him. What I meant of course was a farmer like him, an agricultural general in command of his army of labourers, charging from front to front in his Land Rover to direct the war against nature, and returning home each night to celebrate his victories. In short, I perceived he was a powerful man, and with the slavishness of childhood I identified with his strength even as I shrank from his sarcasm.

There was one way in which I could resolve these Stackpole contradictions, and that was by simply withdrawing myself, the classic child's solution to the insoluble. Towards the end of lunch, as soon as I could gain permission, I would slip out of the dining-room and out of the house, making my way through the office where Raymond, the farm secretary, would be chewing a rancid sandwich amidst the clouds of cigarette smoke that permanently enveloped him. I would run into the yard which at that time was deserted, skip a few desultory stones across the dust and pot-holes, race a stationary tractor or two, manically changing gear and flinging the wheel from side to side, and disappear into one of the buildings. I would push open a crack between the massive doors of the barn that dominated the yard and bore the arms of the Cawdor family in a diamond-shaped shield above its lintel and bury myself among the sacks of grain, turning them into secret dens, hiding places from the Nazis, pillboxes, the tail-guns of bombers, or simply holes where I lay, my mind empty, and would have lain undiscovered for months if the sack mountain above me had collapsed. I would climb the wooden steps to the floor above where the grain was stored loose, and slide like a surfer down the brown slopes, sending up a foam of dust. Once, as I slid to a halt, my shoe uncovered a mouse's nest in which six pink, maggoty babies, blind, formless and not a bit like anything represented by Beatrix Potter, struggled and squirmed.

Sometimes I wandered into the cowsheds to look for

mongrel kittens tamed by the men who fed them milk slopped from the churns in the dairy; sometimes into the sawmill to touch the circular blade with a shrinking finger and feel its jagged, ripping shark's teeth which made the wood scream beneath my bedroom window, or into the tack room beyond the stables to dip my fingers into the groom's barrel and lick off dollops of sticky molasses. Sometimes I went into the mechanic's shop just to sniff the oil, or into the carpenter's shop to fiddle with his chisels, or bang nails into his bench, or squeeze things in his vice.

Of all these places my favourite was the smithy. This blackened, acrid shop stood opposite the house, but its stable door had the great advantage of being invisible from the dining-room window. I was always careful to close it, however, thus immersing myself in a sulphurous twilight, for the only window had long since been furred over with soot. The floor was littered with pieces of metal bric-à-brac – bolts, links of chain, broken tools, bits of shattered hinge, smashed couplings and mysterious chunks of twisted iron, all heaped up in rusting piles round the walls. Standing round the anvil was a collection of hammers, most of them too heavy for me to lift, far less wield. I could, however, manage to swing the smallest and land it on the anvil, where it bounced as if made of rubber but sounded a beautifully clear, ringing note. The forge itself was an enormous brick affair ventilated by a set of leather bellows that would have done service as a whale's lungs. They were worked by means of a long wooden bar with a cow's horn for a handle, and after a few sucking, wheezing strokes the old coals in the forge bed would begin to quiver and glow. I would load on new coal with the long-handled shovel and keep pumping until flames spurted and sparks flew with each gulping breath of the bellows. Still heaving on the cow's horn, I would seize a piece of scrap metal with the pincers, thrust it into the fiercest part of the fire and blast it with heat to the point where it glowed pink and seemed to light up from inside like a piece of stained glass. I would pull it out, lay it on the anvil's horn, bang it into a loop or flatten it like a tongue, and then drop it, sizzling and steaming, into the bucket of water, where its incandescence would instantly die, leaving just another lump of rusting junk. This passage from dross to gem and back to dross again fascinated me, and I would repeat it as often as I dared, always fearing the return of the blacksmith, though he never did catch me.

The men working on the farm must have known what I got up to during their lunch breaks, but they chose to keep a prudent silence and leave the boss's grandson to his own devices, which were, after all, quite harmless. I was not an adventurous child and took no pleasure in destructiveness for its own sake; nor did it ever occur to me to vent my bad feelings, when I had them, in vandalism or any other kind of serious mischief. I was indeed a good boy, to whom obedience and conformity were a way of life. Mine were the solitary games of an only child, more ritualistic than playful, more dream-like than active. They were a kind of narcotic, an escapist trance into which I happily and habitually fell even when the reality of the dining-room was not too irksome.

Concerning one Stackpole activity my feelings were not at all mixed, and that was riding. I hated it.

Somewhere in my parents' collection of photographs is a black-and-white snapshot, taken in the yard at the Home Farm, of my mother astride an enormous horse; she is wearing jodhpurs and a hacking jacket, reminders of the days before the war when she was a keen horsewoman and kept her own mount in the stables. She is smiling broadly at whoever is taking the picture. This would not have been my father; he would have been indoors, sulking, for he disapproved of my mother's riding on grounds of safety. Perched on the horse's neck and caged between my mother's arms is myself, also smiling, though mine is the inane and beatific smile of a small child who knows no better. The picture predates the attack on my nose, and I can be no older than three. It documents the last time I enjoyed sitting on a horse. It probably records too the last time my mother sat in the saddle.

All my mother's family were enthusiastic riders, not to say addicts. My uncle hunted throughout the season, and managed the farm on horseback; later he bred hunters and then racehorses. My two girl cousins, both older than me, were no less fanatical and had their own ponies, which they rode everywhere as town children might ride their bicycles. Indeed Elizabeth, the elder, seemed to me more horse than girl, a sort of female centaur, for I seldom saw her on two legs. And so the day inevitably came when my mother decided that I too should learn to ride and join in the fun. She put me under the charge of Hans, the farm groom, who was a German ex-POW. He addressed me as 'Frizzer', a nickname my mother still occasionally uses, but it proved to be the only concrete legacy of his lessons, because despite the man's best exertions, to say nothing of the pony's, I remained an inept and reluctant pupil.

A couple of years later a second effort was made to get me in the saddle. I was then at the height of my cowboy mania and naively saw myself galloping across the Pembrokeshire prairies, lassoing steers and shooting it out with rustlers. I have a distinct memory from this period of being aboard a horse, wearing my full Western regalia – hat, scarf, sheriff's badge, belt, holsters with strings to tie them to each thigh, and a pair of (plastic) pearl-handled six-guns – but, alas, I also remember being ashamed of the spectacle I made. Notwithstanding his finery, the King of the Cowboys was being led along the lane by his mother and clinging desperately to his pony's mane. In any case, such tomfoolery was not approved of by my grandfather. The era of the Wild West was very shortlived in Stackpole.

Formal lessons were abandoned in favour of my gaining experience, which in practice meant I was saddled up on a pony and left to follow my cousins on their treks round the farm or down to the beach. Off we would go after breakfast, a sedate little trio of junior equestrians, jingling along at a comfortable trot, waved out of the yard by my anxious mother and derisive uncle. Once out of their sight, however, the girls spurred their ponies to a gallop and disappeared with a whoop over the horizon. 'Keep up,' they shouted, their voices growing fainter. My fate then depended on which of two ponies I had been given. Bluebird, a sharp-faced, wild-eyed creature of whom I was terrified, hated to be separated from her stablemates and would race after them, taking no notice of my frantic hauling and jerking on the reins. If I was fortunate, I would be thrown off, freed to walk home with dignity; if not, I would be dragged and bounced in the wake of my cousins for as long as they chose to continue. The other pony, Bessy, was as safe to ride as a sofa, and not much faster, but she took no more notice of my commands than Bluebird. As soon as she was beyond the disciplinary influence of my cousins, especially Elizabeth, who was famous for standing no nonsense from animals, she simply turned round and ambled home, defying all my curses, kicks and heavings at her head.

When it became obvious that I was not a natural rider (or rather, when it became obvious to my mother, for I had known it all along), it was decided that I should, after all, be given lessons during the holidays we spent in Liverpool. This way, it was argued, I would be at less of a disadvantage in respect of my much more proficient cousins, who were able to ride whenever they wished. Accordingly, I was taken on Saturday mornings to a fashionable riding school run by a certain Miss Mahaffey, whose nose was all port and whose voice pure tobacco, but whose seat was beyond reproach. Her lessons were not demanding: we were required to do no more than plod in line, one horse's nose drooping behind the next one's tail, as we circled Liverpool's version of Rotten Row, a sanded track running round Sefton Park. Though I learnt nothing from these sessions, except to avoid Miss Mahaffey's inflamed eye, at least I was safe from humiliation. Or so I thought until one Saturday when my pony, hitherto a model of somnambulism, suddenly reared up on its back legs like Roy Rogers's Trigger, threw me to the ground, and careered down Aigburth Drive out of sight.

To give Miss Mahaffey her due, she was equal to the emergency.

'Bolter!' she cried gleefully and, clamping her hat on her head, gave chase.

By the time she caught up with my runaway steed, or so I was told later, it had succeeded in halting the trams on Aigburth Road, a very busy thoroughfare, and was well on the way to Speke Airport, where perhaps it hoped to make an even more decisive escape.

That afternoon Miss Mahaffey advised my parents that my education as a horseman should be brought to a halt, in her school at any rate.

Around this time another ignominy befell me. During a summer holiday it was decided – by others, of course – that I should join my cousins and enter the local gymkhana. The prospect filled me with dread, and I begged to be allowed to ride Bessy, our docile pony, whose competitive spirit was still more vapid than mine. This was agreed, but at the last minute my cousin Jane, in a fit of contrariness, insisted that she should have Bessy, which would leave me with the treacherous Bluebird. She was given her way.

In the event, although I had no control whatsoever over her performance, Bluebird chose to imitate the other ponies and trotted harmlessly round the arena. However, just as I was beginning to achieve a little confidence, I felt my saddle slipping off her back. I struggled to remain upright, lurched one way then the other, and fell off, my foot still trapped in my stirrup.

At this point I come up against one of those anomalies of childhood that defy adult comprehension. After my downfall, I was intensely ashamed of having given so much amusement to the crowd. I was also smarting from the injustice of the whole episode because I suspected that Bluebird's girth had been the victim of sabotage, or at best a practical joke. And yet, despite these bad feelings, I was intensely proud of the rosette presented to me, on foot, at the end of the day. 'Highly Recommended', it said in silver letters, and I pinned it ostentatiously to my jacket. Indeed, I kept it among my treasures and holy relics for many years.

I cannot remember which of these two catastrophes occurred first, but between them they put paid to my riding career; to my immense relief, it was finally conceded that when it came to horsemanship, I was ineducable. My only regret was that I lost the easiest means of seeing my cousins, who rode almost every day. This feeling was, I am sure, not mutual. They must have been relieved when my riding days were declared officially over because they no longer had to look after me as I traipsed behind them, half-on, half-off my pony, too proud to ask for help, too incompetent to help myself.

Elizabeth was older than me by five years, an almost unbridgeable abyss in childhood, but Jane was only fourteen months older, and as small children we became very close, promising to marry each other in due course. She has since grown into a beautiful woman, and looking back on photographs of us running about on the beach or lined up in our grandparents' garden one can easily see the promise of her beauty in the pretty little girl grimacing at the camera. As a child, one does not notice such things. I only recall our harmonious intimacy, and our seriousness together. Adults, for depressing reasons of their own, often like to see childhood as an era of carefree hilarity and as a result they underestimate the capacity for earnestness which in some children is very strong. Certainly Jane and I, when we were on our own, made an earnest couple. I recall our solemn discussion on the relative advantages of being male and female. To be a boy, she assured me, was much better, because you didn't have to sit down to pee. This and other momentous topics we debated with the gravity of judges. Not that we were always solemn. Although she probably had the merrier temperament, we both found the other's jokes funny. We were, however, much more conversational than playful. Our games, such as they were, did not involve the ever-ramifying creativity that made playing with my friend Anthony in Liverpool so enjoyable, but then Jane and I were ceaselessly absorbed in talk. We shared an untroubled unison. When she laughed, I did; when I was in earnest, she was too; when we grew bored of something, we did so together; we made up our minds as one, and changed them just as inseparably.

This happy communion was not to last. After we had both begun to go away to school, acquiring experience that had nothing in common with each other's and making friends of our own sex who never met, a gap inevitably opened up between us, which in time was widened still further by the introversion of puberty. I remember especially one summer afternoon on the beach when this gap seemed at its most impassable. I looked up from my book – by then I was no longer escaping into the forge or the cow-sheds, but into books – and was astounded to discover Jane *sunbathing*. She was not just lying down to get dry after a swim; she was sunbathing properly, like an adult, deliberately doing nothing but getting brown, with oil all over her arms and legs, and her eyes carefully closed. I had never seen her do this before. Furthermore she was wearing a bikini, a fact I could not help observing, covertly, with a most uncousinly interest. Suddenly, she was no longer Jane;

she was instead a girl, a sexual being, and thus a stranger. In those days (I must have been about fourteen, and she sixteen) all girls were strangers to me, just as I was a stranger – and no doubt strange – to them.

FOUR

When the idea of my being sent to prep school was first
broached to me at the age of eight, I responded positively. Why
not? I knew nothing about it, and could have been persuaded
to go as happily to prison. The prospect of going away from
home and leaving my parents, to say nothing of our dog, the
gross, evil-smelling but much loved Cherry, was unnerving,
but my picture of the school itself was more or less a blank
canvas on which my parents had sketched some vague shapes
in jolly colours, so in a mildly apprehensive spirit I almost
looked forward to my first term. In any case, a sound intuition
told me that for all their show of asking me, this was a decision

my parents had already taken; I was going whether I liked it or not. I settled consequently for liking the idea. My chief concern was over the souvenirs of home I would be allowed to take. Guns, it seemed, were forbidden, and although there was no firm ruling on teddy bears my mother advised me not to take any. Instead, she bought me a small grey rubber mouse of the kind sold in pet shops as toys for cats. This, she explained, I could keep in my pocket without the other boys seeing it.

If my parents took me to view the school before I joined as a pupil, I have forgotten it. Nor do I remember their taking me on my first day, nor their saying goodbye to me, which must have been a heart-wrenching moment on both sides. My first distinct memory of the place is of sitting in a long corridor on a cold linoleum floor, wearing nothing but my dressing gown and underpants and feeling very bewildered. I was in a queue of other boys, none of whom I knew, and I did not know why I was there. No doubt I had been told, but I had not understood. I have never had a strong sense of direction and I was already worried that I would not be able to find the bedroom where I had left my clothes and my mouse. The matron, a most unmotherly person in a white uniform who was known as 'Squawks' on account of her raucous voice, called my name, Harrison, which I did not recognize, and told me it was my turn to see the doctor. A man wearing a stethoscope ordered me to drop my pants, turn my head and cough. After feeling for my balls, an experience that was as uncomfortable as it was unexpected, he pressed his stethoscope against my chest a few times and then, without a word to me, shouted 'Next.'

That night I was too exhausted and bewildered to be homesick. It was a mild September night and darkness had only just closed in as the headmaster said goodnight, switched off the light and closed the door on the bedroom where about ten of us, including one other new boy, were lying in our narrow, metal-framed beds (which for comfort have never been surpassed). A distinctly unmotherly matron had already explained to us 'new-bugs' that we were forbidden to talk or get out of bed after lights out except under dire necessity. The consequence, she warned us, of disobeying this rule would be painful, and she had no need to enlarge on her ominous hint. In my case, her dark threat was doubly redundant, for I was not only timorous, but willingly obedient, and when the rest of the bedroom fell silent, having chorused a squeaky goodnight in reply to the headmaster, it did not occur to me that anything else would be heard from us until the bell rang to wake us in the morning. Beneath the covers I surreptitiously slipped into my mouth the grotesque orthodontic plate I had been given to restrain my buck-toothed top jaw, and, clamped and gagged, composed myself for sleep. To my astonishment, the dutiful silence was suddenly broken.

'Cock fight!' hissed a voice in an excited whisper.

Other voices took up the cry, chanting, 'Cocks! Cocks!'

The darkness was stabbed by the blades of half a dozen torch beams, and boys began to leap from bed to bed, making the springs squeal. Hastily stuffing my ignominious plate under my pillow, I sat up, more thrilled than terrified, to watch the hurdling circus of bodies and their colossal shadows flickering across the walls. A body thumped on to my own bed, but to my relief did not linger. Then the torches converged on one boy, trapping him in their web. He shrieked and tried to crawl under the bed. The others fell on him, yelling, 'Catch the cock!' There was a brief struggle, a muffled plea for mercy, and the race was on again.

I was utterly confused. At first I expected the game to have something to do with imitating farmyard cocks, for I had never heard the word used in any other context. However, instinct and the sense of excitement in the room soon made me realize that these boys, all of whom were as yet nameless strangers, were not playing farms, but a game that was in some way 'rude' or 'dirty'. Even so, I still did not understand what the 'cocks' in question were; nor would I for at least another year, though I had my suspicions. 'Dirty' was the word then used by those in authority, and on occasion by my mother, to condemn what they took to be an unhealthy show of interest in matters lavatorial or sexual, which to young children are of course unintelligibly confused. I was a fastidious child, easily persuaded of the literal as well as moral dirtiness of 'physical functions', but my guilt and repulsion were by no means sufficient to quell my curiosity. I was deeply grateful that I had not been forced to join the game, or, worse, set on as a victim, and I was able therefore to sit watching the participants in a state of appalled fascination.

After a while their energy began to flag. Someone thought he heard a footstep in the corridor outside, and in a flurry of panic the bodies returned to their beds and the torches were doused. The enforced silence gradually gave way to the noisier tranquillity of sleep.

The incident still puzzles me, because I never saw the game played again. As the nights went by and it was not repeated, I thought maybe it was a ritual attached to the first night of term, an excuse as much as anything else to show off newly purchased torches, but many first nights came and went without any mention of cocks, or even a demonstration of battery-powered virility, and after a few terms I stopped expecting it.

I have forgotten when I did finally succumb to homesickness, but it cannot have been long after this lurid introduction to school life. So many strange sensations were rained on us during our first few days that we had no time for any emotions apart from a dazed and fearful bewilderment. However, within a week or so, as faces, objects and rituals gradually acquired a grim familiarity, the true nature of our position began to make itself felt. Out of a mixture of pride and self-protection we all went to great lengths to conceal our feelings, and so I do not know how many other boys suffered from homesickness; I can only say that my own suffering was both acute and chronic.

Like most other boys in their first term, I was utterly

unprepared for the separation from my parents. The longest I had ever spent away from home was a single night, either staying with my Liverpool grandparents, which I did very rarely, or at Leonore's house, which was no more than a hundred yards from my own. Now at school, I missed my parents with an intensity that can only be likened to grief. I felt as if they had died, and the fact that I knew their death was only temporary did nothing to alleviate my sense of loss.

The worst moments came at night. In the darkness and silence it was all too easy to give way to feelings that had been suppressed throughout the busy day, and our dormitories were often disturbed by the sound of muffled sobbing. I seldom cried, but I clung with a desperate passion to the rubber mouse my mother had given me, sneaking it secretly from my pocket to my pillow as I undressed and then clutching it until I fell asleep. It became a totem of my mother and father, a magical creature which possessed their spirit and kept them close to me. I lived in dread of losing it, and woke each morning in a state of wretched anxiety lest it should have disappeared in the night.

I would be dishonest if I gave the impression that these early weeks were passed in a perpetual anguish of longing for home. My temperament was too resilient for that, and our time was too fully occupied. Nevertheless, any little gap in our hectic timetable, any pause that left room for meditation, any little knock, setback or quarrel, would be enough to provoke a terrible pang of unhappiness and remind me of my bereavement. My spirit would be broken again and I would be overtaken by misery, often to my shame under the eyes of other boys. Fighting back tears, I would have to run to some out-of-the-way corner where I could mourn freely for a moment, then gather my strength and try once more to forget my loss.

Homesickness imposes a set of cruel double binds on its victims, and I am sure I still carry the weals inflicted by those prep-school cords. Apart from running away or being expelled, options which no boy took up in my time, there was no instant solution to homesickness. The only cure, and it was a protracted business, was to learn indifference; that is to learn to stop loving your loved ones. Parents should perhaps bear this in mind as they contemplate the crippling fees they will have to stump up for a child's boarding-school education. Along with the no doubt priceless advantages to be had from private schooling, they may be buying their child's estrangement – his emotional frigidity. Here is *their* double bind, and they cannot have it any other way. If he is to survive being sent away from home, he must develop the ability to do without their affection, at least for the time being. And to achieve this he must either cease to feel any affection on his side or split himself off from his feelings, suspending them until they can be allowed to flow painlessly again. It is this alienation from feeling that is the most destructive legacy of the boarding-school years. However, children do not have an aptitude for stolidity, which is hardly surprising since their whole upbringing to the day of their being dispatched to school will have been designed to bring on their natural capacity for loving. From their earliest years they are taught to love their parents, their brothers and sisters and everyone else within range, and it would be a hard and exceptional parent indeed who, in order to train his son for the rigours of prep school, taught him to keep his love on a leash and hold his family in only tepid regard.

In fairness, it has to be said that parents too are obliged to forgo and disguise their feelings. My parents, I know, found our partings harrowing, and my mother, from whom I had after all been a constant companion for nearly nine years, was especially distressed. But for my sake she had to mask her emotions, for nothing would have upset and embarrassed me more than the sight of her weeping as we said goodbye in the school yard or on the station platform. She too had to suffer a wedge being driven between her feelings and her behaviour, though in her case the hammer was of her own making.

The double bind did not end here; it was a python with many more coils. In later years, when these things were at last discussed, my parents asked me why on earth I did not tell them of my homesickness at the time, and why I did not complain of the other aspects of the school, notably being beaten, which I found irksome. It is true that I said nothing and gave no inkling of my unhappiness in my letters, but my parents were the last people to whom I would have complained if I had ever thought of doing so. For one thing, I was too frightened of them. They had, after all, sent me away from home, which was bad enough; what might they do to me if I made a fuss? It could only be worse. And anyway I wanted to please, not to irritate them. To complain would surely be to offend them, and that would alienate the only people on whom I could rely to protect me. For were they not my sole source of love, which distance and deprivation had rendered all the more precious? I was not going to put this at risk by bellyaching about the arrangements they had made for me. In any case, what was the point of telling them anything? They could not change what went on inside the school, and they were hardly going to take me out of it. And so on and so forth; round and round. I yearned for the company of the very people who had banished me, and yet I was frightened of losing their love by telling them how much I needed it.

Of course, being a child, I lacked the analytical powers, to say nothing of the words, to spell out these dilemmas to myself; I simply languished in confusion. It is in the nature of a double bind that the dilemma does not let you see it for what it is. When you are caught in its coils, you can see neither head nor tail; you only feel its sinuous grip squeezing the life out of you.

As a boarding-school child, you were not only separated from your parents, but in your homesickness you were isolated from everyone else too. To seek comfort from the staff was out of the question. None of them looked at all approachable, while Squawks, the only visible woman, was positively forbidding. And it was obvious that they would not be sympathetic to someone who longed to escape from them and their horrible institution. Nor was it possible to confide in another boy; at least, I never did so. To begin with, you had no friends whom you could trust, but in any case you quickly learnt that no one was more despised than a 'blubber', a boy who broke the prevailing code of stoicism. It would have been deeply shaming to admit that you wanted your mother and would have made you very vulnerable. In fact, there was next to no bullying in the school, but that perhaps only showed how effective the code was. Our stoicism required no promotion by the staff; it was one of those unwritten and virtually unspoken mores which nevertheless is fully understood by each member of the community. Everyone's self-respect was at stake: if one boy blubbed, the others would be poignantly reminded of their own unhappiness and brought dangerously close to blubbing themselves. He had therefore to be repressed at all costs. For most of us, who had been raised in families where every little worry was drawn out and soothed, this was the beginning of that process by which our feelings were first numbed and then disconnnected, giving us the distinctive quality of the boarding-school 'man'. At all events, I am sure something vital was killed off inside me during this period which I have never been able to revive.

In the long run, the most wounding of all these new experiences was the realization that you were not wanted at home by those whom you loved most; in the short term, the one feeling that sliced through the great knot of confusion in which you were entangled was the simple aching desire to be back with your mum and dad. Sunday was the worst day of the week, because it contained so many intervals of empty time which could not be crossed without thinking of home, and it is no coincidence that the next day I remember clearly from my first term was our first Sunday.

Sunday was the slowest day of the week unless your parents came to visit; then it was the quickest, which in a way was worse. It was also the day we were required to write our letters home. Before sealing them up, we had to show our efforts to the master on duty, a precaution taken in the name of good spelling and punctuation, though it was presumably a security measure too. I never read another boy's letters, but mine certainly posed no threat to the school's reputation, except perhaps by way of being dull.

Dear Mummy and Daddy,
How are you? I am well. I played football yesterday. I nearly scored a goal. I sit next to Bailey 11. Please send me a cake . . .

After lunch on this first Sunday it was explained to us as new boys that we had to go to the scullery and collect our issue of one potato, two slices of bread and two matches. We were then supposed to disappear into the grounds below the house, known as 'Long Bounds', and amuse ourselves for the rest of the afternoon. We had already been shown this narrow strip of wild woodland running along the precipitous bank of a stony, gurgling stream, and it looked quite terrifying. It was made more sinister by the thick clumps of bamboo that grew among the ordinary trees.

Long Bounds was penetrated by a labyrinth of paths, in which I knew I would get lost. No one had told me what I was meant to do with my potato, bread and matches, so I put them in my pocket and proceeded fearfully down the widest and most frequented path. I had overheard rumours of gangs who gathered on Sundays to ambush new boys and throw them in the nettle beds, of which, I observed with horror, there were a great many, all emerald-ripe with stinging poison. I had even heard that they captured their victims, tied them up and flogged them with nettle whips.

The bush was infested with whooping, crashing boys. Suddenly my path was blocked.

'Lend us your matches. I'll pay you back next week.'

I gladly surrendered them.

'Thanks. What's your name?'

'Fra . . . Harrison, I mean.'

'Jolly good.' He disappeared.

After wandering about for a while, I came across a large fire surrounded by a crowd of boys, none of whom seemed likely to be nettle-whippers, and so I joined them. Nobody paid any attention to me, which was just the sort of acceptance I had hoped for. I pulled out of my pocket what remained of my slice of bread and, copying the others, put it on a stick to hold it in front of the fire. It blackened rapidly without even getting warm, but when I tried it the taste was delicious. I rolled my potato into the ash and never saw it again, for it became instantly indistinguishable from the lumps of charcoal heaped round it.

I wandered some more, moving from fire to fire, and then, quite without warning, I was overtaken by diarrhoea. I knew that if I did not get back to the school at once I was going to humiliate myself dreadfully. I ran as fast as I could while yet struggling to control my fulminating bowels. I soon became lost and began to cry, which did not improve my powers of navigation. Inevitably, the worst occurred and, stumbling wetly through the jungle, I knew I would have to present myself to the dreaded Squawks, smelling and unsightly.

Memory has drawn a fastidious curtain over the latter stages of this ignominious episode.

Whenever my parents described the school they would always wax lyrical over the beauty of its grounds. Last year, after a gap of nearly thirty years, I returned to the school site and discovered, as if for the first time, that this was indeed true: the place was a Welsh paradise. I walked down from the house, past the ornamental garden where we were made to act a Shakespeare play each summer, and into the woods high above the glittering stream. My only thought was, 'If only the children were with me, how much they would enjoy this.' It was not until I paused to sit on a little stone bridge that the irony of my reaction struck me. I had assumed exactly what my parents had assumed; and reasonably so, for the place was, or ought to have been, a perfect playground for small children. It was not only beautiful, but wonderfully adapted for exploring and adventuring, for making camps and simply messing about. But homesickness, alas, is a great killjoy, and this splendid playground was never anything to me except a barbarous place of exile. And by the time I had outgrown homesickness my tastes in Sunday afternoon amusement did not include playing at pioneers, or anything that smacked even remotely of scouting, which I had come to hate.

I was to be ill with diarrhoea during much of that first term, and because of the chagrin it entailed, more than any physical discomfort, it was a source of considerable misery to me. Thanks to a system that appeared to have been devised entirely for the purposes of degradation, it was impossible for a new boy to suffer discreetly from indigestion. After breakfast and before morning prayers the whole school gathered in the hall and adjoining classroom to do its prep, and during this period boys were allowed on the basis of a rota to visit the lavatories. One set of doorless stalls was situated beyond the boot room, while another, the more favoured, was concealed amidst an obscure grove of trees set beyond the stable yard and beyond the view of all but the most officious staff. A trip to these far-flung bogs gave ample opportunity for loitering and gossip. New boys, however, had to submit themselves to a very different and much less clubbable arrangement, known as 'Supervision'. They were instructed to go upstairs and queue outside Matron's dispensary, next to which was a gleaming white, surgically immaculate facility. Each boy was made to closet himself in turn and perform as quickly and as best he could. But on pain of dire punishment, he was not permitted to pull the chain. Instead, he had to stand by the door while Matron inspected his achievement and then inscribed the results in a large, leather-bound register. She must, I suppose, have used some code to distinguish between the categories of stool she reviewed every morning, but I was always too mortified to want to see what she wrote down.

If the matron ever wearied of this seemingly repulsive duty, she showed no sign of it but conducted herself with the same awesome gusto morning after morning. Whenever the object of her scrutiny was defective in some way, remedial medicine was issued on the spot and the miscreant was required to present himself for an extra, post-luncheon inspection; if things had still not improved he would be placed on a thrice-daily course of supervision. For shy children, unused to having these functions mentioned, far less examined and documented, the matron's morning roll-call was an ordeal indeed.

Later in the term my digestive misfortunes took a decisive turn. The sweet chestnuts ripened, and, showing perhaps the first sign of what was to become a lethally addictive temperament, I devoted every possible moment to eating these nuts and cramming my pockets with illicit supplies. We were permitted to collect them for roasting on Sundays, but eating them indoors was forbidden on account of the mess caused by the shells. I could not wait to roast mine, and ate them raw, which is still the way I prefer them. My fragile stomach soon rebelled against the huge quantities of hardly-skinned nuts I inflicted on it, and I fell ill; so ill in fact that I put myself beyond the recording powers of even Squawks's Domesday register and had to be consigned to the sanatorium. Here, for the first time, I was at ease, if not actually happy. For the first time in twelve weeks I was safely beyond the reach of threatening masters, threatening rules and, most debilitating of all, the constant threat of being beaten. Squawks did not decline so far as to be motherly, but she did at least sheathe her sharpest blade, and for as long as I was an official invalid treated me in a way that was dimly reminiscent of home.

It would be histrionic to call this episode a 'breakdown', but I am sure there was more to it than a simple over-indulgence in chestnuts. I had had enough of the school, and without realizing it, certainly without consciously planning it, had retreated into illness. Once I had recovered, I never suffered from chronic diarrhoea again; or if I did, it became my business alone, because the following term I was taken off the dreaded Supervision list.

FIVE

As a result of my 'accident' in the woods, I probably spent my first Sunday evening in bed, in which case I would have missed what proved to be one of the highlights of the week – the Sunday reading by the headmaster. Hitherto he had presented himself as an altogether terrifying figure, but when I saw him seated in a large leather armchair, his glasses on the end of his nose, with the entire school gathered round him, he seemed for a moment benign and avuncular. Sprawling on the floor, perched on windowsills and piled up like logs in the corners of the hall, we listened with rapt attention as he read, for he read extremely well. His choice of books was strictly confined to the

74

nineteenth-century classics – Stevenson, Kipling, Macaulay (*The Lays of Ancient Rome*), Conan Doyle and Dickens – Dickens, above all.

I do not know whether he used versions of these books adapted for children; I think not, because again and again in later life I found myself recognizing quotations from novels of Dickens which I had never read. Not only scenes and characters but turns of phrase as well had lodged themselves in my mind. The headmaster must have possessed remarkable powers as a reader to have held our interest during those many passages which, as I have discovered while trying to introduce my own children to Dickens, are not readily intelligible to eight-year-old ears. He had the makings of a talented actor, too, for he was blessed with a fine voice that was both musical and versatile, and he could impersonate Miss Trotwood and Little Em'ly, Oliver and Fagin, with equal conviction.

It was perhaps this ability to act that made him in every other respect a frightening character, almost a Dickensian invention, himself. In truth he was, I suspect, a kindly if unimaginative man, but having cast himself as headmaster he was determined to play it whole-heartedly. The role he chose was that of Dr Arnold, naturally, although he could not resist rewriting it a little to accommodate a hint of Mr Wackford Squeers. In appearance he was handsome in a rugged, high-coloured way, with a hero's tough jaw and short, straight nose. His hair was black and grew in youthful curls. All the boys' mothers flirted with him at speech days. His eyes were blue, of course, and they met yours in a stare that was as unflinching as his handshake was crushing. He was a rugger blue and a convinced Christian, which placed him squarely – he could never have been placed at any other angle – in the tradition of muscular Christian educationalists. In manner, however, he was more regal than priestly. For all his preaching about modesty and humility to us, he himself obviously relished those moments in the school timetable when he could stand over our abjectly bowed heads, his academic gown and hood spread magnificently behind him, and issue his diktats.

I write now with an adult's sense of irony, and in retrospect it is easy to see the humbuggery that went into his performance, but as a child I was utterly convinced by his show of majesty. I took the mask to be the man, and it frightened me, as it frightened all of us.

The philosophy of the school was the hadmaster's, and though it was very much of its time, it bore his distinctive stamp by being simply expressed and vigorously executed. His ideas were drawn mostly from Baden-Powell, but were sanctified by the Bible and stiffened with a touch of Kurt Hahn's spartanism. Thus we were divided into scout patrols rather than houses, and all our achievements, sporting and academic, were alleged to redound to the glory of the patrol. I found myself a Swift, as opposed to a Curlew, Plover or Owl, and in due course was elected, by a modest majority, to be leader of my patrol in my last term.

At every turn there was a strong and declared emphasis on character-building. The repeated use of this expression suggested that our characters, as delivered to the school by our despairing parents, were so many sacks of cement and heaps of bricks which, left to themselves, would never amount to more than ugly rubble. It seemed it was the job of the great architect our headmaster and his team of master-builders to turn us into sound, morally waterproof little dwellings, with roofs strong enough to resist the rains of temptation from without, and dampcourses to secure us against corruption from within.

And so, in the name of character-building, we were made to undergo all kinds of physical indignity and discomfort. Foremost among these ordeals was the early-morning summer swim. During the second half of the summer term regardless of weather or temperature, we were woken half an hour earlier than usual and paraded in front of the house. The headmaster counted our drooping heads and then led us in a crocodile towards the lake. Under ordinary conditions, this was a pleasant stroll of two or three hundred yards across a meadow, but on these summer mornings it turned into a via dolorosa, for we were forbidden to wear shoes or any clothing apart from our 'bathers'. With towels clutched around our scrawny shoulders, we shivered, yawned and hopped our way through the icy, dew-drenched grass. The headmaster himself, whose character by then was presumably upright enough to need no further building, was wisely clad in sweaters, overcoat, and wellington boots with thick socks turned snugly over their tops. If the weather was unusually cold, he wound his college scarf round his neck, and when it rained he protected himself beneath a large, multicoloured umbrella whose shelter we were not permitted to share. In any case, he heartily strode ahead of his limping, quaking charges, urging them on with threats and empty promises. Finally, we gathered in a miserable, trembling crowd around a small landing stage, whose rotting feet were sunk in the gelid mud below one of the lake's steeper banks. Here the headmaster took up his position, armed with a long pole which he would thrust in the direction of any boy in danger of drowning. The more robust and philosophical boys entered the arctic water voluntarily, some running off the landing stage and hurling themselves in with suicidal screams, others creeping with masochistic caution into the black ooze. But, lingering wretchedly on the brink, there was always a small knot of incorrigible cowards, myself among them, who had to be coerced.

'In with you,' the headmaster would shout at us, poking his pole at our shrinking bodies.

'Buck up, Harrison. It's warmer in than out.' To prove his point, he banged his arms round his chest to keep up his own circulation.

Persistent reluctance was rewarded with a wellington boot in the backside, which propelled the craven victim into the water with a whimpering splash.

Despite these dreaded expeditions, I did learn to swim with some proficiency, and even came to enjoy it. Rugger, on the other hand, I hated in all its forms and on all occasions. The game was rendered all the more loathsome by that touch of sadism, that insistence on avoidable suffering inflicted for the alleged good of our characters, which characterized the school's ideology. Soccer, which I enjoyed in a galumphing, goalless fashion, was played in the milder autumn term, but rugger was reserved for the short, raw afternoons of the winter term when the climate was at its most punitive. As in the case of our summer swimming, the weather was not allowed to interfere with the dictates of the timetable, and on days allotted to rugger, come blizzard, frost or fog, we were marched in shuddering, purple-nosed files down the drive towards the playing fields. Only rain, providing it fell with the strength of a monsoon, would keep us indoors, our reprieve being signalled by the posting of a crabbed notice, glumly pinned to the board by the headmaster and deliriously received by all but the most bovine and sycophantic boys, stating that games were regretfully cancelled for the afternoon.

Under ordinary, ice-bound conditions, we were driven mercilessly to our doom, our studs ringing with the same grim peal on the adamantine grass as on the metal road. We pulled off our sweaters, piled them in a sodden heap on the touch-line – for it was strictly forbidden to wear them during play or even practice – and shambled listlessly on to the pitch. The headmaster, appropriately dressed once again in his thickest overcoat and longest scarf, gave us our positions and divided us into teams, which were expected to feel instant and ferocious enmity for each other. I was usually posted to play on the wing, saved by my skinny ribcage from the gladiatorial horrors of the scrum. Hovering on the edge of the mêlée, I would run about with an eager, loping action which was, I hoped, eloquent of an urgent desire to be in the thick of the game. I would earnestly chase the boy with the ball at a safe but inconspicuous distance, occasionally making futile lunges at his shadow though never committing myself to an actual tackle. My intention was to give a display of heroic ineptitude, thus winning approval for effort, while disguising my complete lack of participation in the fray. Some traces of mud on the knees was essential to this charade, which I strengthened with groans of disappointment and yells of frustration when the ball appeared to elude me. I became extremely artful in this form of theatre, and would often pass whole games without ever touching the ball or coming into abrasive contact with another boy. It was not an easy feat to perform, because the headmaster did not confine himself to the touch-line but lumbered after the focus of play, shouting advice and abuse. In fact, he was obliged to join us on the pitch, visibility generally being so bad that we would simply have disappeared into the freezing murk had he not pursued us. Thankfully, he was almost always satisfied with a show of endeavour, no matter how unprofitable to the score, for in his eyes the greatest crime a boy could commit on the rugby field was not ineffectiveness but 'funk'.

Now and again I was put in the scrum, and then there was nothing for it but to submit to one's punishment, though I was always amazed by those thick-skinned, bullet-headed boys who did not just go through the motions, leaning without pushing and scrabbling to avoid rather than collect the ball, as I did, but who apparently relished having their ears rubbed off and their skulls cracked.

Still worse, however, was the torment of tackling practice, which by a twist of perverse logic we were forced to endure when the ground was judged too hard for a proper game to be played. We were separated into pairs and, under the choleric scrutiny of the headmaster, took turns in bringing each other down by means of a 'fair tackle'. This consisted of making a horizontal dive in order to grasp one's sprinting, high-kicking victim round the knees and send both bodies crashing on to the

79

cast-iron turf. Only the most dim-witted boys threw themselves into these kamikaze missions; the rest would try to get
away with collaring their partners round the neck or waist,
which allowed both to roll more or less painlessly to the floor.
But such effeminacy was not tolerated.

'Foul tackle!' the headmaster would shout furiously at the
guilty pair. 'Do it again.'

Another fumbling attempt would be made.

'Tackle him *low*. This is rugby football, not pat-a-cake.'

His insults and aphorisms were repeated, word for word, at
every practice, invariably raising a thin titter from his audience, though this was not the effect he intended. To do him
justice, he never played to the gallery, as other masters did.
Brandishing his umbrella in genuine outrage at the decadence
he saw all around him, he coined his catch-phrases with a fresh
passion each time.

'Hold him by the knees, boy. Don't hang round his neck.
What are you trying to do, dance with him?'

'Take your man cleanly,' he would shout, as another couple
of small boys made their stumbling run into the mist.

'That's more like it. Now, Harrison, let's see what you're
made of.'

And so the afternoon would pass in agony and boredom,
our hands and feet losing all feeling in the cold, our numbed
minds concentrating only on the hardly imaginable moment
when the headmaster would at last look at his watch and –
reluctantly – blow his whistle, pointing towards the house and
the swampy, tepid baths that awaited us. Trudging home in
the half-dark, my sweater now too dank to afford any warmth,
I felt a sense not just of physical misery, but of despair as well.

At such times homesickness tore at the entrails. There was,
however, one other situation in which it attacked still more
acutely, and that was towards the end of my parents' weekend
visits. These took place during the autumn and summer terms
and I looked forward to them with an almost visionary

anticipation. Exeat lasted from Saturday lunch-time until Sunday evening, though boys had to spend the night in school and be present for prayers on Sunday morning. Parents were always welcome to attend, but mine never did and I never encouraged them. The visits passed in a whirl of treats and gorging at hotels and teashops. When I was older and had made friends, I usually took another boy with me to join in the orgy. As often as not I invited (David) Bailey 11, a most agreeable boy who went on like me to Shrewsbury, and he would take me out in return. His home was nearby, so an exeat with him meant playing in his garden, eating in his kitchen with his mum and dad, and generally leading an ordinary family life for a few hours. But during my first few terms my parents' visits were too precious to share with anyone else. They usually stayed at a hotel on the coast, a baronial affair with a dining-room overlooking the sea and a mighty, Gothic, stone edifice in the hall which resembled the tomb of some great man but was in fact a humble fireplace. In my mother's eyes, the great virtue of this hotel was that it obligingly served high tea in the early evening, allowing her to see me stuff myself to the gills before the time appointed for delivering me back to school. To my mind its best asset was its so-called Games Room, actually a ballroom in which a single table-tennis table had been installed for the amusement of the many small boys and their parents who kept the place in business out of season. Here my father and I played whole tournaments of ping-pong on wet afternoons. In the summer we would go down to the shore and skim stones across the rock pools, a skill at which we were both adept. These are very warm memories.

But on Sunday evenings, looming over us all, was the prospect of my ever more imminent return to school. My parents' cases were brought down from their room, my father paid the bill, my mother fussed anxiously over my last-minute requests, and we got into the car. As we drove along the narrow, hedge-bound, twisting lanes that led to the school gates, I would fall quiet, unable to think of anything but the coming agony of parting. Sitting alone in the back, I hoped my distress was not being noticed, for I was frightened of upsetting my parents and I had my pride. Nonetheless, I felt an anguish on those return journeys I have very seldom felt since, and then only when being parted from someone else.

It was a relief when the school gates appeared at last and we drove the final few hundred yards up the winding, pot-holed drive. We parked in the cobbled yard at the back of the house. I kissed my mother, shook hands with my father, thanked them both for a wizard weekend and rushed inside. The ordeal was virtually over now, for it was easy to be absorbed by the familiar noise and chaos of the school having its cocoa, and there remained only the final testing minutes of the weekend when the lights were turned out and I was alone in the dark, adding up the weeks that were left before the end of term.

SIX

On and off the pitch, the headmaster was altogether a daunting figure, for he was not only the absolute monarch of our little kingdom, but our father as well. The teaching staff consisted entirely of men, with the single, bewitching exception of the music mistress, of whom more later, and although there were other women about the place, working in the kitchens and bedrooms, they slaved under the pitiless eye of Squawks, whose icy frown withered up any show of female softness even as it bloomed. This then was the head-master's one-sided family and he was its super-father. His rule was not mollified by the influence, far less the counter-authority (to which many of us were used at home) of a mother figure. His wife, a gentle and sensitive woman by all accounts, played no part in our existence, except to provide an ethereally gracious presence at our functions and ceremonials. So the headmaster stood over us like a glowering Jehovah, a single arbitrary authority whose laws allowed no appeal, whose wrath was far more dreadful than any ordinary father's, whose vengeance was swift and sure, and whose baleful eye could see directly into the murkiest corners of our consciences. It goes without saying that we lived in mortal terror of him.

His manner was awe-inspiring enough, but he made his authority utterly secure by the simple device of reserving to himself alone the power to judge our crimes and administer punishment. Ordinary discipline was maintained by a system of nuisance points which were posted on a large chart displayed in the main corridor. Minor infractions of the many laws that dogged our behaviour were punishable with blue stars, more serious offences with red stars, and truly heinous offences with black stars. These were awarded by the junior masters who inscribed them on the chart with the appropriate crayon. The purpose of the system was to provide a series of precarious second chances before the persistent criminal was finally condemned to his fate – a visit to the headmaster's study. Masters always had the option of sending boys immediately to see the headmaster, but they only did so after detecting a crime of almost unthinkable wickedness or daring, such as cheating or climbing the clock tower. To be sent to the headmaster under these circumstances meant a certain caning. Usually, however, they preferred to play the points game, which at least gave the victim a sporting chance of escape, for a boy had to accumulate three blue stars, two reds or one black before he was required to present himself to the headmaster, an obligation he was on his honour to fulfil.

These measures were designed to suppress the usual boyish

wrongdoings: running in the corridors, talking when forbidden, sliding on the polished wooden floors, climbing out of windows, lateness, scruffiness, rowdiness, inattentiveness, untidiness, cheekiness, and so on. But only a boarding school, whose inmates are both powerless and imprisoned, could elevate such petty vexations into crimes and then burden the criminals with an elaborate penal system which punished the mind far more cruelly than the body.

A few masters disdained to use the system altogether, preferring to retain some small authority of their own. Take, for example, Muldoon, the classics master. He was a short, shoulderless man whose huge, elongated head rose out of his collar like a bristled column. He was extremely unstable, and was given to violent twitching when angered. Even in repose his face was continually disturbed with little tics and flutters causing his eyebrows to box at each other like hares and his lips to jive in ghastly, meaningless grins. He also mumbled continuously to himself, as if in life and death debate with an evil spirit. He was easily riled, and when he supervised our morning prep it was our sport to provoke one of his spectacular losses of temper.

'Please, sir, there's an elephant in the garden.'

'Don't be stupid, boy. Get on with your work.'

'There is, sir, honestly. Do you think we should tell the police?'

'Did Hannibal use African or Indian elephants, sir?'

'Ugh! It's made a frightful mess on the lawn.'

Suddenly his face would flush purple, his twitching would become seismic, he would grind his teeth audibly, his eyes would bulge, his lips would foam and he would begin to rant and bellow.

'Sit . . . Desks . . . Books . . . Get out . . . Corridor . . .'

We would sit cowering and sniggering while he fought to gain control of his rage. His struggle was terrible to watch, but in time his colour would fade to its customary mottle, his hectic pacing would become slower and his speech would once more be coherent. And yet, despite our shameless taunting and the obviously desperate ordeal we put him through, which seemed to bring him to the very brink of mass homicide, he never resorted to the points system. His rages, though impressive, were not really frightening; having detonated him, we would sit quietly watching, awed but not apprehensive, as if observing a volcano from a safe distance. We knew he was his own enemy, not ours. He was in fact more dangerous when simmering than exploding, for he was wickedly accurate at clipping across the top of an unsuspecting skull with his flattened hand and nearly opening it up like a boiled egg.

Of all the masters in the school, he was, oddly enough, the most liked, and some boys, realizing that a warped brilliance lay beneath the hysteria, even came to revere him. This same turbulence, when directed outwards, turned him into a teacher with a unique ability of bringing a historical scene to life before your very eyes. I can see him now, sweating and grunting as he loaded imaginary boulders into a Roman catapult, winding its twisted thongs just short of breaking point before firing its mighty fusillade, which whistled through the air and pulverized the barbarian hordes. I can see him bent double with one hairy arm raised as he held up his shield to form a testudo with the other soldiers in his century, and I can hear the enemy's spears rattling on his shell of shields as he advanced inexorably on their standard.

Mr Smuts, by contrast, was feared and despised. At first sight, he appeared to possess the right qualities to impress small boys. He was tall and spare, with the look of the desert about him, his eyes seeming more accustomed to shimmering mirages and horizonless wastes of sand than rows of desks and muddy touch-lines. He was said to have been a secret agent during the war, a rumour that was confirmed to our satisfaction by the murderous-looking dirk he wore tucked into his sock as an exotic addition to his scoutmaster's uniform. He was an excellent shot with a rifle, a sharp-eyed naturalist, and a fair hand at ping-pong, which he played holding his bat handle in a sophisticated grip more suited to a pen but borrowed, so he assured us, from the Chinese. He also wore a narrow, perfectly clipped moustache above his bloodless lip, a manly embellishment which was alleged to stir Squawks's libido to a passionate froth.

But although he boasted these heroic attributes, he was universally disliked. Far from living up to his dashing reputation as a secret agent, he behaved more like a secret policeman, specializing in the surprise arrest. Padding silently across the floorboards in his rubber-soled brothel creepers, he would mark out his victim and stealthily approach from behind until he was standing directly over the unwitting boy, who was, let us say, mirthfully telling a smutty story ('vulgarity' was considered a very serious offence). The boy's audience would fall silent, fascinated and horrified as he prattled on in hilarious ignorance, while Smuts would gather himself for the strike, swaying slightly from side to side like a cobra. Then, faster than the eye could follow, he would seize the wretched felon by the short hairs at the back of his neck and march him in public disgrace to the punishment board. How he seemed to love those stars and their combinations of pain and anxiety; how finely he seemed to calculate the misery he inflicted. And what profound satisfaction he seemed to derive from the humiliations he was able to exact by means of his simple but deadly sarcasm.

'What is your name?' I remember his asking of a boy, whose name of course he knew perfectly well.

'Wright, sir,' pronounced the guilty one, glumly.

'Wright!' He seemed hardly able to credit it. 'Wright? Are you sure?'

'Yes, sir, Wright.'

'Well, we must call you Wrong from now on, because that's what you are – a wrong 'un.'

His Wildean cracks would be greeted with howls of laughter from the craven, traitorous bystanders, and the utter crushing of his prey would be complete. In reality, of course, these were howls of relief that it was not they but some other poor wretch who was the object of his persecution. I wonder if he ever realized that.

And so, once the dreaded combination of nuisance points had been acquired, the malefactor was doomed to make his confession to the headmaster. Getting to see him was by no means a straightforward matter, because he did not hold his judicial sessions every day, but only on a Monday, Wednesday and Friday. The implications of this staggered timetable could be devastating. If, for example, you took your collection of stars over the fateful total by sniggering during prayers on a Monday morning, just after that day's hearings had finished, you would have no choice but to stew in terrified anticipation throughout a whole forty-eight hours – two long days and two still longer nights. Worse yet, if you were caught and condemned on a Friday morning, you would not only have an extra day to wait, but you would also have to endure the many hours of the weekend that were arid with free time and left the mind free to brood exclusively on what was to happen. The very worst scenario occurred if this was a weekend when your parents came to visit, for then the most cherished pleasure the term had to offer would be turned to ashes. I wonder if these permutations of unhappiness occurred to the headmaster when he devised his system.

When at last the day came for reporting to the headmaster, you made your way to his study, slowly or hastily according to your temperament, during the period immediately after break-fast when the others were doing their prep and enjoying the dubious amusements of the bogs. His study lay at the end of a large, airy corridor that led past the dining-room and kitchens and was reached by way of a small, lightless lobby. Here a crowd of would-be confessors queued and quaked, their ears pressed to the heavy mahogany door in an effort to gauge the heat of the old man's temper. There was much jockeying for places in the line, some wanting to get it over with, others nursing a misplaced belief that leniency prevailed towards the end.

The door opens. The criminal emerges, rubbing his bottom, tears on his face.

'He's in a terrible bate. Good luck.'

You knock.

'Come.'

A push from behind and you enter.

'Well, Harrison? I'm sorry to see you here.'

You stand on the carpet in front of his desk, trembling and unable to speak for fear of blubbing.

'Speak up, boy.'

'Mr Smuts gave me a black star for playing football in the hall.'

His face darkens with irritation.

'When?'

'During break on Friday.'

'You know that's forbidden. The football pitch is the proper place for football. I will not allow this house to be taken over by hooligans.'

'Yes, sir, but it was only a paper ball, and I wasn't the only one.'

'Don't tell me tales, Harrison. You are an intelligent boy and too old for these silly tricks. I shall have to beat you. You know that, don't you?'

'Yes, sir.'

'Bend over, then. Go on, bend right over.'

He points to the all-too-familiar black leather chair and you crouch over its arm, smelling the frayed skin and horsehair. Peering backwards, you can just see him picking up the slipper and drawing back his jacket sleeve to expose a dense mat of black hair on his thick arm.

'Get your head down. I don't want to find you here again.'

His arm goes back, comes down, and a terrific report rings out. The pain is in fact not too bad, but the shock is terrible. Crying now, out of relief and humiliation, you retire from the room. You are overwhelmed with shame.

It would be wrong to suggest that these beatings in themselves were anything other than mild. Even when administering the cane, which he did very rarely, the headmaster was never brutal, and, within his own, entirely arbitrary code, he was always fair. After a 'whacking' with the slipper, a scarlet mark, or at the worst a faint bruise, was all that we ever discovered in our eager examinations later. But the beating, such as it was, did not constitute the real punishment. We were punished much more by the elaborate ritual that surrounded the whole business from the moment our stars were recorded on the board. The damage was done long before we reached that grim study door, and the beauty of it was that we inflicted it on ourselves. During those hours and days of fearful expectation we beat ourselves a thousand times over, and we did so far harder than the headmaster himself would ever have dared.

And when we finally reached the study, the actual beating was nothing compared with the agony of waiting beforehand in the lobby, the humiliation of confessing to trivial acts of mischief that were made to seem deeply shameful, the sheer helplessness of knowing that no extenuation would be listened to and no excuse accepted, and, most pernicious of all, the degradation of abasing ourselves, bottoms-up, to the clinical wrath of a father figure who, only minutes later, would be preaching to us the virtues of charity, forgiveness and brotherly love.

I don't suppose my school was any better or worse in this respect than others of its type and period. It was just ordinarily damaging. I have often heard the parents of children sent to these schools pooh-pooh any accusation of sadism. While implying that it is contemptibly wet of anyone to suggest such a thing, they defend the men and their system on the grounds that no lasting harm was done to us, that we were taught a valuable lesson in discipline which has stood us in good stead in later life, and that even if our mentors were a little short on imagination, they were committing no crime worse than the use of old-fashioned methods. And anyway, they add jovially, what's so wrong with the occasional smack with a slipper? In our day, it was always the cane, and plenty of it, and what was good enough for us . . .

By 'old-fashioned', they mean to say that these methods were not deliberately cruel, but simply ones sanctified by tradition and applied, perhaps thoughtlessly, by traditional men. But this is not the point, for in a child's eyes the method and the man are never separate. It is the man who beats you and the method is his, wherever he got it from. Our parents did not seem to realize that these headmasters, whom by and large they despised, notwithstanding the huge sums of money they put into their pockets, were not only our teachers, our gaolers and persecutors, but, for the time being, our parents as well. I do not think it far-fetched to suggest that one of the reasons relations between boarding-school sons and their fathers so often develop badly is that the men who stood in for their fathers were unlovable, and in some cases actually cruel or brutal. The nature of their job perhaps demands that head-masters should be unlovable, but parents overlook the fact that their sons are bound to look to these men to replace what they have temporarily lost. The bitterness that always follows an unrequited love is rendered all the more poisonous when it is brought home and transferred to the true father, who naturally feels puzzled and unjustly condemned.

Throughout my prep- and public-school years I never met any man, apart from my father, for whom I felt real respect, with the single exception of my English teacher at Shrewsbury, 'Willy' Jones, and I did not get to know him until my last couple of terms. For the rest of the men who dealt with me I felt either fear or, at the best, an amused indifference. This was not healthy. Children, especially sons, need good father figures no less than they need good fathers: men who can act as models to imitate and even heroes to look up to. In some families the role is played by uncles, in some by the father's friends, though these were not available in my case. To be continually in the company of 'bad' father figures, as I was, undoubtedly has a destructive effect, for it not only spoils the core relationship with the father at home, but has a damaging long-term impact on the son's image of himself as a man and father.

As to discipline, I don't think I was taught any habits of learning or codes of behaviour that I could not have learnt at a good day school, and would not have learnt just as readily at my prep-school without the perpetual threat of being beaten. The question of character-building is more ticklish. I do possess a certain self-sufficiency (of a strictly sedentary and cerebral kind) which probably owes more to my prep school training that I care to admit. However, I am sure that in other respects the school's admittedly mild brand of spartanism, far from toughening me up, made me resolutely wet. I might have enjoyed the place more if homesickness had not turned its petty discomforts into terrible privations, and indeed if my home had not been so very comfortable. As it was, every pang of hunger, every stab of cold and every twinge of pain served to remind me that I was in exile, and soon enough I came to loathe all those activities that exposed me to the slightest physical distress. To this day I regard the outdoors with the gravest suspicion and positively abhor all forms of exercise.

Homesickness continued to plague me for more terms than was usual or dignified. Like a cold-weather malaria, it had infected my bloodstream, and returned again and again to lay me low. In a sense, I have never been cured. Looking back on the whole sorry business, I am convinced that the rift which has divided me from my parents, and especially from my father, was first cracked open by the shock of my being sent away to school. Of course, as the years went by, even I became inured to the endless round of separation and reunion that makes up the calendar of any child at boarding school, but as this happened the rift between us became settled, a fixed feature of our relationship. In the meantime, another fissure had opened up, a crack within my mind, which split it like a geological fault from the crust to the very core of my being. I became – and still am – a divided person, and although I have sometimes managed to seal over the gap, it has never been a true join. From between the lips of this unhealable wound a poisonous lava continually leaks. My character was built, all right, but not in the shape of a tidy, upright residence. By the time my teachers had finished with me, I was a ramshackle, subsiding shack which had been constructed over this volatile breach in my mind, and I have spent the rest of my life trying to prop it up and keep it stable.

SEVEN

Like most of the other boys at school, I was an insatiable reader, though I never mastered the art of reading comfortably down my bed by the light of a torch. As might be expected, by far the most popular genre of book among us was the adventure story, with which our little library was generously stocked. I vividly remember the row of broad, stout spines, each with its own inspiring illustration in colour, of the novels of G.A. Henty. I often took them down, attracted to their pictures of stirring action and to the periods of history promised in their titles – *With Clive in India, Under Drake's Flag*, and so forth. Their imperialist heroics and racist paternalism, far from being objectionable, were exactly what I hoped to find, but despite these allurements I could never finish them, for I found myself becoming bogged down in military technicalities – action was what we craved – and a prose style which seemed too difficult after the racy simplicity of writers describing our most recent war.

In my first terms, I preferred the innocent thrills provided by Enid Blyton through her Adventurous Four, a sort of senior branch of the Famous Five. The Four involved themselves in escapades very much to my taste, and I especially recall a high-wire rescue calling for a teetering walk above a foaming torrent in order to reach a castle tower; memory, probably working too hard, has added a parrot to the acrobatic hero's shoulder. In those days I longed to own a parrot.

At about the age of ten, seeking to compensate for the family I had lost, I liked books in which the characters got together in groups to have their adventures, mutually supporting each other and fostering eccentricity. For this reason Biggles appealed to me. I was not much interested in planes, even in every boy's favourite, the Spitfire, though I did enjoy the dogfights we waged out on the lawn, holding our arms wide as we ran about making zooming noises punctuated by the staccato of our machine guns. Nor did I identify with Biggles's brand of square-jawed pugnacity. What I appreciated was the camaraderie of the squadron room, where the friendships between Algy, Ginger, Tug and their revered squadron leader flourished in amiable pranks and banter. These motherless families of men, with their decent leaders and daring exploits, were bound to hold a special appeal for small boys in our situation, for they represented a gloriously enhanced version of our own inglorious orphanhood. I found Billy Bunter stories enjoyable for the same reason. The deceits and indignities of the Fat Owl himself were mildly amusing, but my real pleasure lay in being able to become a vicarious member of the Remove alongside the clean-limbed Bob Cherry and the rest of Bunter's colourful classmates.

We identified still more keenly with another kind of book, the prisoner-of-war story, an sub-genre of war literature which was being created at that time as ex-POWs began to write about their experiences. Dog-eared paperback copies of *Boldness Be My Friend, The White Rabbit, The Wooden Horse, Escape From Colditz*, Douglas Bader's *Reach For The Sky*, and so forth were passed round ('Bags me after you, Harrison') and avidly read until they fell apart. The most shocking, and most impatiently queued for, were those written by survivors of Japanese camps, notably *The Naked Island* by Russel Braddon with illustrations by Ronald Searle. I have not looked at the book since, nor visited Searle's recent exhibition of war drawings, but I remember very clearly his picture of an exhausted British soldier being made to hold a large rock above his head for the amusement of leering Japanese guards, one of whom, leaning back in his chair, prods the prisoner's back with a sharpened bamboo stick. It was not until many years later that I realized this was the same Searle who had written and drawn the Molesworth diaries, books which were unanimously acclaimed at my prep school as the funniest our literature could possibly offer.

The POW books were best-sellers in those days, but they possessed an extra fascination for us because the way of life they described, particularly in the milder German camps, seemed to mirror our own imprisonment so closely. We had no difficulty in identifying with the continual cold, hunger and other privations suffered by the inmates of the *Stalags*. Christmas concerts, food parcels and secret conferences after lights out, homesickness and the terror of punishment, persecution at the hands of sadistic 'goons', interrrogations in the commandant's office ('I will only give my name, rank and number. God save the King!') and life-saving dreams of escape were all too easy for us to imagine.

We also had another, more complicated and less savoury interest in these books. Published one after another during the early 'fifties, they revealed to the British public for the first time the details of what had been suffered in German and Japanese camps, and we were therefore reading them in the atmosphere of horror and outrage which they aroused. Yet, though we shared these feelings, our response was also coloured by a certain relish for their stories of torture and brutality. No doubt all boys of that age share an overheated fascination about such things, but we were in an unusual position. Having been born in the early and mid 'forties, we were the first generation to have no memories of our own of the war in which our fathers had fought, and so it is not surprising that we read these accounts of manhood, our fathers' manhood, being put to the test with very mixed emotions.

It is often said that boys are aggressive and destructive, if not downright sadistic, but although we were strongly drawn to this new literature of cruelty, our reaction to it was fraught with a confusing masochism, especially when we came to read scenes of sexual maltreatment. Two incidents drawn from these books stand out in my memory as being more discussed and ruminated upon than any others, and both involve sexual humiliation. One, which I think appeared in *The White Rabbit* by Bruce Marshall, described the author's being forced to run naked between two rows of jeering female guards; he was then taken to a shower room and half-drowned in icy water in a vain effort to make him talk. We were far more horrified (and intrigued) by his humiliation than his pain, for his ordeal was an acting out not only of our fears, but our desires as well. Without realizing it, we had discovered the ambiguous nature of sex: while we were terrified of having our burgeoning virility laughed at, we were just as eager to display it, especially to an audience of rapt, anonymous women.

The second incident shows up this ambiguity still more clearly, and here I mistrust my memory, because I cannot relate it to a particular book and suspect it was a fantasy concocted derivatively from our reading rather than drawn from a specific account. At any rate, true or not, it was the subject of much hysterical speculation among us and even more meditation in private. Some British soldiers were tied naked to a line of stakes and compelled at bayonet point to watch as a bevy of nubile native girls danced lasciviously in front of them and taunted their enforced celibacy. Furthermore – and here is the touch of Gothic eroticism which I suspect we added ourselves – an electrified wire was stretched before the victims, just below waist height; this carried a massive voltage and when touched by erect tissue would cause sudden death.

Apart from the fact that this scenario seems improbable on practical grounds, since to be effective it requires the use of men of exactly the same height, to say nothing of length, I doubt its authenticity because its sadistic dilemma embodies so precisely our pubescent anxieties and longings. Perfectly condensed in the ecstasy and agony of this torture was our fear that sexuality was in some way fatally dangerous while also being uncontrollably compulsive. The beginnings of the aching frustration that torments and bewilders adolescence were registered in this histrionic marriage of lust and guilt, and it was an expression of wish-fulfilment too, for in the absence of any experience or understanding of how sexual relations were to be arranged, our fantasies were all dependent on fantasy women taking the initiative and turning us into half-willing, half-resisting subjects. We longed to be tempted, though we feared the temptation and could not imagine the temptress. The striptease dancer, and behind her the prostitute, were already beckoning.

This concern with tumescence and its dangers dates the fantasy, in my case, to my last year at prep school. I vividly recall walking into the bathroom ('the swills') one evening after

98

games and looking down to discover, much to my astonishment, a feathery crown of black hair, which appeared to have sprouted between my legs that very day. And I have a separate memory, located in the bathroom at home, of realizing for the first time that the pleasant and familiar extension with which I was playing had a formal title: I had become the author of 'an erection'. To endow my old friend with this scientific status was to render it both foreign and formidable.

Despite these intriguing developments, my knowledge of sexual relations remained half-baked, and my attitude to the whole business was one of prudish disdain. One evening, as I was standing in a queue waiting to recite irregular verbs to the headmaster, the boy next to me said, 'Do you know what fuck is?' He spoke in a doleful tone, and his question was evidently the product of extensive and sorrowful meditation.

'What?' I could hardly believe my ears.

'You know. Fuck.' He made a complicated gesture, which did not enlighten me. 'Do you know what it means?'

'Yes, of course,' I replied, quite untruthfully. I had heard the word no more than once or twice, for it was not among my parents' vocabulary of swear-words, or at any rate not among the ones they used in my hearing. Beyond knowing that it was unmentionable and 'dirty' I had no idea of its specific meaning.

'It's what your dad does to your mum,' he explained, perceiving my ignorance.

Now I was really disgusted. It was certainly not what *my* dad did to *my* mum. And yet I knew he was right.

'They do it at night,' he added, and sighed. The subject was clearly a source of distress to him, and I can only guess at the agonies of private speculation and anxiety that had led him to initiate the conversation with me, for though I cannot recall his face or name, I know he was not one of my friends and confidants.

I turned away priggishly, leaving him to his melancholy brooding.

It was not that I did not know how babies were made.
Thanks to my mother's patient and informative replies to my
oft-repeated enquiries into that fascinating topic, I had a fair
understanding, for my age, of the process and its mechanics.
But like most children, I was far less interested in sex, as such,
than in the almost fabulous story of my own origins as a
growing entity in the womb. This boy had shocked me by
giving a name – a horrible, ugly name, it seemed to me – to
something which hitherto I had never considered in isolation,
never thought of as an activity in its own right with its own
separate label. It had merely been the first incident – 'The
daddy puts his penis into the mummy' – in the unfolding
drama of life before birth, to which the daddy of the fairy-tale
contributed nothing of importance, certainly nothing worthy
of a special verb. An irregular verb if ever there was one.

We were given lessons in reproduction, but as far as I recall
they were of the birds and bees variety, and the mating habits
of human beings were not mentioned. We were left to draw the
inference for ourselves. I may be wrong, but if human sexuality
was in fact included in this branch of natural history, I can
never have listened with much attention for I was smugly
conscious of already knowing all about it. I looked with
contempt on the knots of sniggering boys who gathered after [1]
these lessons to share their incredulity and voice their ludicrous theories.

'Not up their bottoms, stupid! They have a special hole.'
'Where?'
'Where they piss, I think.'
'Ugh.'
Endowed with my great fund of expertise, I could afford to
laugh at these troglodytes. It was of course another hole
altogether. A virgina. Hence the word *virgin*. (What exactly
was a virgin?) The thought of this spaghetti-junction of
plumbing lodged within the female trunk was not an easy one
to accept; it was, however, an entirely abstract conundrum,

quite dissociated from any real, flesh-and-blood woman or any woman I knew. The idea of, say, Granny having a virgina was, well, inconceivable, and rather revolting.

On the other hand, I was not wholly confident of the knowledge I possessed, though I would never have confessed my doubts either to a friend or to my mother. I was too proud to admit to even the smallest air-pocket in my omniscience, and the age of innocent, unselfconscious questioning had for me long since passed. And so I puzzled in solitary bewilderment over the gaps and anomalies in my version of the Facts of Life. One Fact I had got hopelessly wrong, for example, was the difference between sperm and urine. Never having experienced an orgasm (an all-important Fact, which is usually omitted from the explanations offered to children), I assumed that when the daddy had put his ... etc., he despatched the seed on its voyage by doing a sort of pee inside the mummy. As a result, I would often stand in the 'bog' beyond the boot room staring with wonderment – and a little anxiety – at the stream of what I understood to be baby-seeds gushing wastefully down the urinal wall. I imagined them struggling blindly to fulfil their destiny while they drowned in the school's sewage system. I had been told that millions of them were produced at a time, and the spectacle of these numberless hordes of my children, dead before they were alive, splashing twice or thrice daily down the cracked and stained channel of a common jakes was worrying, though I marvelled at my inexhaustible springs of fertility.

To return to the war: it played a far more influential role in our upbringing than we knew, and perhaps it had a greater influence on our educators' methods than they themselves appreciated. Although our scouting system placed a heavier emphasis on parades, uniforms, ranking, survival skills, codes of honour and other pseudo-soldierly activities than the ordinary house system, there was nothing explicitly militaristic or bellicose in our school's regimen. However, our scouting and the general stress on self-reliance, physical stoicism and respect for hierarchy did add up to a sort of unacknowledged preparation, if not for the next war, at any rate for the next national crisis, in which we would be required to do our bit, just as all the adults in charge of us had recently done theirs in the war itself. Our teachers' sense of impending emergency was by no means fanciful, for the Korean War had been in active progress, with British soldiers dying in battle, in 1953, the year I first went to the school. It was entirely reasonable for them to anticipate that in due course their pupils would at the least be conscripted into national service. They were not to know that conscription was soon to be cancelled, in 1960, an event which reduced our corps training at public school to a repugnant farce.

As a result of this atmosphere, we grew up with a feeling of responsibility for the way the world turned; or rather we inherited our elders' assumption that as ordinary people we would be summoned to intervene in the making (and correcting) of history. This was both a legacy of the war and a last spasm of the imperialist delusion, which even as we imbibed it was being outmoded by the 'winds of change'. It is the inescapable lot of children to receive attitudes that are already decaying into obsolescence, and in our case these included the notion of Britain's moral as well as material supremacy. As we grew up, we were of course disillusioned, becoming the first generation to see a positive value in the retreat from imperialism. On the other hand, I believe we never shed our parents' assumption that the fate of the world could be affected by our ideas and efforts. That was our tragedy. The fact that young people nowadays know that the world is impervious to idealism is theirs.

My generation has been spared the duty of fighting a war, and in the unlikely event of the next war being conducted across old-fashioned front lines and battlefields we will be too old to be of any use. We have saved our own skins, but then we may still bequeath the worst war of all to our children. However, when our turn came in the 'sixties we did fight other kinds of battle, some of which look foolish now, others self-indulgent, and others still, notably the Campaign for Nuclear Disarmament in its first phase, tragic for having proved so ineffectual. Futile or not, all these campaigns and protests, all these movements and creeds which we generated with such fertility were consistent in one respect: they were panaceas, cure-alls, universal solutions. Our dreams were millenarian, our politics revolutionary, our religions transcendental and our pleasures Utopian. We were nothing if not cosmic in our thinking, and for this I am sure we have our parents' generation to thank, because they taught us, by example and inference, to believe that like them we had an obligation to rescue the world from its enemies. Our means of salvation were very different to theirs, and mostly repellent to them, but our basic principles were not altogether dissimilar and they shared a common origin in the war's heritage.

Of the war itself we knew next to nothing, and we were to learn very little more during the remainder of our education; indeed, the whole of the twentieth century failed to get itself on any history curriculum I was ever taught. When I left my prep school I was thoroughly versed in the arts of besieging and defending medieval castles, and by the time I left my public school I was a positive expert on the campaigns of Cromwell, Marlborough and Wellington. To this day, relying only on an unrefreshed memory, I could draw up a plan of battle manoeuvres at Trafalgar. But as far as Alamein, Pearl Harbor, Operation Overlord, the Battle of the Bulge and the rest were concerned, they were barely names to me, and anything I knew about them was derived from films, not books, and certainly not from lessons. I could recite the causes of the Seven Years' War as glibly as my French irregular verbs, yet the causes of the war in which my own father, to say nothing of many of my teachers, had fought, went unexplained and unmentioned. For all our fevered reading of POW books, we were quite ignorant about every aspect of the war except its result. We the British had stood alone, defying the might of the Hun, and thanks to the genius of our leader, Churchill, we had triumphed. It was called a world war because we had taken on the rest of the world. The idea that we had been helped never occurred to us, and we would have greeted the suggestion that our allies, the Americans and the Russians, had if anything contributed more than we had to the victory as a vicious blasphemy. And yet there were some puzzling elements in my understanding of these events. If the war was fought against Germany and therefore, presumably, on German soil, what was my father doing in Africa? And why did he fight his bit of the war in shorts, with a monkey on his shoulder, surrounded by grinning black men also in shorts?

In the eyes of their children, parents who are out at work all day are at once so familiar that they are of no interest, and so mysterious that they confound curiosity. Their jobs, above all, are utterly beyond comprehension, and when explained are meaningless. I had no idea what my father did all day; all I knew was that he wore a bowler hat and a black suit, carried a briefcase to and from the bus stop, and sat in 'the office'. When I was old enough, I was allowed to run down our street to the main road in the evenings and meet his bus. So well regulated were his days that I never had to wait for more than a few minutes. His way of life, in so far as I thought about it, seemed enviable to me, especially since I was very fond of riding on buses. He generally left the house in high spirits and returned in the same mood. If he brought worries home from the office, as no doubt he did, he concealed them from me. Without throwing any light on the inscrutable nature of his work, our jolly walks back to the house did give me the impression that whatever his job was it provided him with satisfaction and amusement, which was indeed the case.

Oddly enough, I had a far more informed notion of his life during the war before I was born than I had of his daily routine at the office. While serving in West Africa – for him, though I only learnt this later, a miserable and debilitating sentence – he had sent home to my mother a great many photographs of himself, and when I became old enough to be interested she showed them to me, telling me the story of his war and hers. They were of course the small, square, black-and-white snaps of those days, the product of the then universal Kodak 'Brownie' camera, and their chiaroscuro had been made all the more extreme by the fierce sunlight in which they had been taken. Smiling jauntily in each one was a thin, pale, round-faced young man who sported a dashing moustache and was only remotely recognizable as my father.

I was intensely proud of the fact that he was a captain, though my pride was somewhat misplaced since I confused his rank with its naval namesake, and I was prouder still of the exotic locale of his war. There he stood (admittedly in those regrettable shorts), secured in the album of my memory, his swagger stick under his arm, his faithful black bodyguard at his side, with the African sun beating down on his curling moustache. If his function in the war fought by Bader, the Dam Busters, Churchill and the others was difficult to understand, his status as superman was unimpaired: he was the Great White Chief, the bwana of bwanas. No other boy of my acquaintance could boast a father who had ever set foot on the Dark Continent, far less won the war there, and none could boast a father with a monkey for a pet. My father himself seldom spoke of his adventures in West Africa, largely because he had had very few, but I was soon able to replace his reticence with my own mythology. Shortly after arriving at prep school I read Edgar Wallace's *Sanders of the River*, which is set in a fictional version of Nigeria, and I immediately adopted Sanders's exploits as my father's. I don't know whether people, boys or otherwise, read these Sanders books nowadays, or even whether they are still in print. Their racism, casual sadism and British chauvinism would get them automatically proscribed by those educational authorities who believe in literary laundering of this kind, but in my day the only books forbidden to us were those containing sexual descriptions thought too explicit for our innocent eyes. This was a policy designed more to sedate than to protect us, but I am sure it never occurred to the headmaster that whereas our libidos were unlikely to be kept dormant by being denied *The Cruel Sea* and other allegedly pornographic works, our racial prejudices would almost certainly have proved less intractable in later, adult life if our reading of these 'wog-bashing' classics had been more closely supervised.

The most vivid image I had of my father in Africa, which was directly derived from the Sanders stories, was of him seated in the prow of a dug-out canoe, his pith helmet on his head, his cocked revolver in his hand, and his eyes raking the jungle bank for signs of hostile natives. Behind him the shining black backs of his myrmidons were bent over their paddles, and as they sped through the green, crocodile-infested waters my father led them in singing their battle chant. This improbable fantasy was as sharply realized in my imagination as a portrait in a locket. Like most childhood fantasies it was a highly charged and visionary reworking of prosaic fact, and in this case I am certain the concrete memory being celebrated was that of my father singing to me in his bath, which was a regular feature of our weekends. I loved to sit in the water with him, as my children do with me, and while we rowed together down the Niger of Aigburth Hall Avenue (much to my mother's annoyance, for our river was always in full flood), he would chant in his distinctive, tuneless voice his versions of the African work songs he had learnt during the war.

Once I was at school these songs became magic incantations which I would croon to myself, conjuring up both the steamy, enveloping warmth of home and the invincible power of my warrior-father. His songs were my blues, the hymns of my defiance, and I never sang them more lustily than during our so-called music lessons. Once a week we were required to gather round the grand piano in the big hall and grind our way through a book of folk-songs. Nothing in our curriculum bored me more, and under cover of the noise made by the other boys as they wailed and roared the words of 'Clementine', 'The Lincolnshire Poacher', 'There is a tavern in the town', and so forth (songs I rather relish now), I would apply my own tuneless voice to a subversive rendition of my father's bath-time repertoire. During my periods of homesickness, I derived much comfort from these private, underground concerts, which always allowed me to escape our grim Welsh fortress and drift downstream into that jungle-bound domain where, in the guise of my father, I was the dauntless Massa, feared by my enemies, loved by my subjects.

I should add that these classes, though musically unrewarding, were not altogether tiresome, for our singing, if that is the word, was directed by a mistress, the only one working in the school, whose figure was by common consent inflammatorily seductive. As we assembled for her class and before she entered the room, we competed fiercely for position, not at the back but at the front, nearest her piano, and when she joined us she commanded the most obsequious obedience. The object of this jockeying and servility was to gain a place from which one could enjoy a clear view of her *décolletage*. She was always modestly dressed, but favoured blouses buttoned up the front, which, as she threw herself into playing the rollicking choruses of her favourite tunes, would strain against her splendid bosom and occasionally, to our pop-eyed delight, spring open to disclose an inch or two of pink, mobile cleavage. There were boys who claimed they had even glimpsed her nipple, a phenomenon as rare and fabulous to us as an eclipse of the sun or the abominable snowman, but jealousy and scepticism saw to it that these sightings were never credited. The other women who worked in the school, with the exception of a pretty under-matron whose career with us was mysteriously short-lived, were dispossessed of any sexual charisma by age or simple ugliness, and so the hour-glass music mistress was indeed the sole mistress of our voyeuristic cravings.

She could hardly have been unaware of our fervid concentration on her demure front, but she never acknowledged it. She neither flaunted herself nor made any effort to disrupt our collective ogle; she seemed neither to relish nor to resent our attentions. Her mellow shape aroused ambivalent feelings in us: she was a living reminder of motherly softness, even of milky infancy, and at the same time she was a promise of sensual adventures which, though scarcely conceivable in practice, were already intoxicating to contemplate. Her enigmatic aloofness from the effects of her physical presence was also our first lesson in the puzzle of lust. Did she know how she excited us? Was she excitable herself? Were girls the same in this respect as boys, or if different, in what way? For those of us whose social contact with girls was too restricted for this puzzle to be explained, the music mistress was the first in a long series of objects of desire, untouchable and unapproachable, who unwittingly pointed the way to Simone's door.

EIGHT

In due course I reached the age when my parents had to decide
where to send me next. They had my name down for a number
of schools, including Sedbergh, my paternal grandfather's
Alma Mater. He had in fact hated being there, but applying the
quaint traditionalist principle of what was bad for me will be
good for my son he had arranged for my father to follow him.
In the event, ill health had prevented my father from going,
and so my grandfather had to wait until my turn came round
before trying again to establish a family succession at the
place. Fortunately for me, my mother had heard somewhere
that Sedbergh was notorious for its harsh regime of cold baths,

long runs and the absolute prohibition of vests even in the cruellest weather, and she vetoed his choice; it was one of the few occasions when my parents defied his wishes head-on. After making a visit of inspection and liking the school for its own sake as well as for its proximity to Liverpool, they chose to send me to Shrewsbury. I am glad they did so.

First, however, I had to pass the Common Entrance exam. There was no talk of my being scholarship material now; indeed I must have been in an academic slump, because my results were awaited with trepidation and everyone was relieved to find that I had just made the grade. If I left my prep school with any pangs of regret, I have forgotten them. Nor do I even recall what was said by the headmaster during his long-anticipated 'leavers' talk'. As part of the bizarre conspiracy by which it was then thought proper to shroud all sexual matters in secrecy, the leavers themselves were solemnly bound by a vow of silence to impart not a word of these talks to their juniors, and of course they kept their vow, though more out of meanness than principle. Much wild and fanciful speculation was attached to the 'talks' and the mystery was further deepened by the fact that they were held in the dead of night. The general consensus was that the headmaster offered technical advice, with the aid of graphic illustrations culled from books written by Frenchmen, concerning one's wedding night – in short, he told the leavers how to do 'it'. I believe that in reality he warned us of the evils of masturbation and the still greater evils of homosexuality, which we might be invited to practise at our public schools. Never having masturbated and having no concrete idea of what was involved, I listened to his warnings in bewildered disappointment, and promptly forgot all about them.

For some reason I started my career at Shrewsbury in the summer term of 1958, rather than in the autumn term at the beginning of the academic year. On a sunny May afternoon my parents drove me with my trunk and tuck-box to join the other boys and their luggage at Ridgemount House. We were met by the housemaster, a man of imposing corpulence, who had once been a fine oarsman and had since run to a mighty stoutness. He was not so much fat as thick in all parts, and resembled a bifurcate barrel. His voice was low and guttural, his balding head was invariably oiled with a patina of anxious sweat, and, as I discovered that day, his nickname was 'Butch'. He offered to give my parents tea, but said he was sure I would want to be with the rest of the house.

He opened a door and ushered me through. The room was quite dark except for the spectral light of a television whose black-and-white glow illuminated row upon row of intent faces. The boys were watching a football match and seemed tremendously concerned about its outcome. I had never seen a football match on television before, nor heard of the Cup Final, which was what it proved to be. Though I was both confused and bored, I had the wisdom to conceal my ignorance and keep quiet until it was finished.

Parting from my parents was only briefly painful, for I was eager to get into the swim of this new institution, this new home. I was put in the charge of an older 'scum' – the Salopian term for fag – who showed me my bedroom and study. Wingfield explained that I was to be his responsibility for the next two weeks, and that he would be punished for any crimes I might commit during that period. But he made it clear that such punishment as he did suffer on my behalf would be passed on, with interest. His chief task, apart from acting as escort and guide, was to coach me in the 'colour test', a catechism of school rules and names of places on the site, which would be mercilessly conducted by the monitors in three weeks' time. As he was telling me what would be the horrible consequences – for both of us, but especially for me – of my failing this test, a noise like an air-raid siren, a drawn-out wail rising gradually up the scale, penetrated the corridors, and was followed by a stampeding of feet from all corners of the house. Grabbing my arm, my minder rushed me in the direction of this unearthly cry.

'Dowel call,' he said meaninglessly as we ran.

Rounding a corner, we skidded into a crowd of small boys milling about a much larger boy, who was forcing out the last few seconds of his summons.

'Shit!' said my minder. 'We're the last. The last one gets the job.'

But just as the monitor was finally running out of breath, a boy whose face was inflamed with eczema clattered down the stairs and stood ruefully at the edge of the mob.

'Welcome back to house, Scott,' said the monitor, elegantly. 'Bring my boxes in, will you. And don't drop them.'

Scott muttered something under his breath.

'I didn't quite catch that, Scott,' the monitor remarked in a tone of silky menace.

'I'm going, I'm going,' mumbled Morris in a marked Manchester accent, and plodded down the corridor, glowering but silent.

'The Scratcher's always last. Too busy scratching himself. Spastic anus.'

The rest of the scum dispersed. The monitor, who was almost twice the height of the smallest boys, sauntered into the front yard, and as he watched the Scratcher struggling with his luggage he whistled quietly to himself, his hands in his pockets.

Wingfield pointed derisively at him.

'Look at him, the lazy tit. But don't you stand there. The lawn's for monitors only. And don't put your hands in your pockets on the school site. You've got to be here two years before you can do that.'

We continued our tour of inspection. He took me across the yard and showed me a noxious lavatory block, a set of fetid changing-rooms and a swampish bathhouse equipped with a line of cold-water showers and two huge, grimy tubs. Back in the house he took me round the studies, each of which was furnished with a single broken-down armchair. Every boy had a desk and a set of shelves to himself. These were made of oak which had been hacked and carved and stained, and the grain of all the desk lids had been scored in deep grooves. Beyond the studies was a so-called new extension which contained a games room, where a few boys were already engrossed in a snooker match played on a table whose baize was greasy with use, and a library, where Wingfield drew my attention with some pride to a battered set of Ian Fleming novels. Finally, he took me to the dining hall, showed me the house 'pots' (silver cups), and told me there was a scullery beyond where we might make tea and toast in the afternoons.

'Don't poke the maids,' he said cheerfully, 'or you'll be thrown out.'

Then he abandoned me, returning to find me at strategic moments to take me into supper and so on. He was a tall, raw-boned, genial boy who did not seem to resent having to shepherd me, and I was grateful for his attentions.

At seven o'clock the bell at the bottom of the stairs was rung and Wingfield told me I had to go upstairs with the rest of the new scum. Exhausted, I was soon in bed, trying to make myself inconspicuous. Another new boy lay beside me, but we did not speak. The room held a dozen more beds and seemed huge. While we lay there, vulnerable and helpless – we had been told it was against the rules for us to get out of bed – we were made the objects of inspection by older boys, who put their heads round the door, smirked and guffawed, and went away. There was talk of 'tea-boys' and 'luscious new scum', but evidently we did not fit the bill, and without really knowing what we had escaped we were relieved to be left alone with our books.

Every half-hour the bell would ring again, bringing another wave of boys upstairs, until all the beds were occupied; the monitor in charge of us strolled in last, wearing a stylish silk dressing gown. The housemaster stood for a moment in the doorway, grunted a salutation which was returned without enthusiasm, and put out the light.

Although I came from a home fastidiously furnished and decorated by my mother, who abhorred the slightest sign of untidiness or 'grubbiness', I was not bothered, still less disgusted, by the shabby squalor of my new surroundings, which made my prep school look like a classy hotel. Conditions at Shrewsbury were in accordance with the strange English principle decreeing that the older the school, the more illustrious its name and the more exorbitant its fees, the slummier its facilities and the fouler its food should be. Only one aspect of the school seriously disturbed me, and that was the bullying, or rather the teasing, which some unfortunate boys were made to suffer and which I feared would be turned on me. I never saw anyone bullied in the classic style of *Tom Brown's Schooldays*, which I had, perhaps mistakenly, read as preparation in the holidays before my arrival. We new scum were not tossed in blankets, nor roasted over fires, and there was no Flashman waiting to brutalize us. On the other hand, the place was rife with teasing and name-calling which went to vicious lengths; or so it seemed to me, for there had been nothing like it at my prep school. There, only one boy had been maltreated to the point of regular tearfulness, and he was a neatness fanatic who kept the contents of his desk in such a state of neurotic orderliness that it posed an irresistible temptation to the rest of us. Time and again, the wretched child would open the lid of his desk only to discover that his meticulously graded piles of exercise books and pencil boxes had been reduced to rubble. And then, to the gleeful satisfaction of his molesters, he would invariably 'blub'.

At Shrewsbury, nobody seemed to escape being tagged by some mildly abusive nickname, usually derived with crude wit from a play on his surname or from a physical peculiarity. Thus

Morgan was known inevitably as 'Organ', while another boy
who was prone to shaving his hair well back above his ears,
was dubbed 'the Monk'. These names were used with affection
or malice as occasion dictated. But certain boys were cruelly
persecuted with their nicknames. The cruelty lay in unweary-
ing reiteration. The Scratcher, for example, could never enter a
room without hearing a mocking reference to his unfortunate
condition. Sometimes he was also called 'Mucky Scratcher'
out of contempt for his scruffiness. Yet he appeared to cope
with all this uncomplainingly. He had a robustly morose
temperament, and at first I thought he was only relieved that
his harassment was not more severe. I was wrong. One day,
when the two of us were alone, I made the mistake of
addressing him as 'Scratch'; not out of any desire to insult him,
but simply out of thoughtless familiarity. He turned on me
and, with a furious vehemence that took me completely by
surprise, said, 'Don't ever call me that again, you lifty
(impertinent) little twat, or I'll tear your balls off.'

I did not need warning twice.

There was another boy in our house who was teased, but
who lacked the strength to retaliate even against those younger
than himself, and the memory of his persecution haunts me
still. Owing to his unusually bloodless complexion and
cadaverous physique, he was known as 'Corpse', and whenever he passed we would pretend to shiver, rolling our eyes in
mock terror and making ghoulish noises. He was also known
as 'Bones', which prompted us to rattle invisible skeletons in
his face and click our teeth at him like animated skulls. These
rituals were performed as casual reflex actions rather than
gestures of calculated malice, but they were the invariable
greeting he met with wherever he went and whatever he said,
which was precious little. He was two years older than I, and
by the time I joined the house he had been teased so
unremittingly that he had been forced to imprison himself in a
cage of silence, a sort of open solitary confinement. In an effort

to efface himself and avoid attracting further torment, he had taken his nickname one stage further: he was more ghostly than corpse-like, and no longer lived in the house but haunted it, creeping elusively along its edges, never speaking or looking at anyone, his pale eyes hidden in their hollow sockets. I never saw a boy so lonely.

It may be thought I am exaggerating, but only those who have been to institutions where there is no retreat at nights to the consolation of home and the support of family, where the staff, without wishing to encourage cruelty, are insensitive to the emotional needs of their charges, and where there is a powerful ethic of stoicism in the face of suffering and a savage hatred of 'sneaking', can ever understand the completeness of Bones's isolation. I am ashamed to say that although I was horrified by his plight, I still added my voice to those of his regular torturers. I had a glib and facetious tongue which I did not hesitate to use in the cause of self-promotion.

There were of course plenty of boys who were not persecuted, and plenty of others who developed stratagems for keeping would-be persecutors at bay. One of the most bizarre, and misconceived, was dreamt up by a boy roughly my age. His name was McDuff, which naturally earned him the sparklingly imaginative nickname of McDuffer, soon shortened to Duffer, but he was further handicapped by a sharp Edinburgh accent which guaranteed that he was almost perpetually mimicked. He could not open his mouth without having his every word echoed in a mincing, Jean Brodie-ish voice, and wherever he went he was pursued by a moronic litany of 'och ayes', 'hoots mons', and so forth.

Duffer turned out to have a jovial temperament and more strength of character, or rather eccentricity, than anyone expected. He took his teasing in good part and seemed to think of it as a rough-and-ready expression of acceptance. He rapidly acquired a widespread notoriety rare in a new scum, because he was mischievous and could never resist the kind of stunt that would bring him publicity. He was also very easily led, as my old friend Tom and I soon discovered, and could be put up to the most foolish escapades, for which he would take his punishment without complaint or any resentment at our having egged him on. If a bread-pellet fight got under way during a meal, he could be relied on to take things too far, throwing the bread instead of flicking it, and hurling lumps, or even whole rounds, until he made himself so obvious that he was caught. Then, as the wrath of authority descended on him, he would grin slyly at us, acknowledging our silent applause. As he grew older, his mischief turned into delinquency, but he lost none of his old exhibitionism. Not for him the furtive visits to the cinema or the clandestine smoking sessions which the rest of us screwed up our courage to enjoy; these crimes were far too covert for his taste. He would get drunk on Saturday afternoons, swigging openly from the bottle in his study and then throwing up for good measure. Finally, there was a scandal over a maid, whom he used to kiss in full view of the house on summer evenings, and he did not return to school the following term.

Despite his accent he was a voluble talker, and during his first year he found the teasing which greeted his every remark very frustrating. Indeed, he became so exasperated that he resorted to an alternative mode of articulation, one which he brought to a fine pitch of expressiveness: he took to farting. I have never heard farts since to compare with his. They were explosively loud, yet not without musical qualities, and strangely odourless. Most remarkable of all was his ability to play his instrument at will, and his timing was always spot-on. For example, when the whole house was gathered in the hall to do its evening prep and every head was bowed in silent concentration, he would release one of his most reverberant chords. Needless to say, his performances were always hilariously received by the rest of us, and he needed no encouragement to give us an encore.

His tricks were soon quelled by the monitors, who simply threatened him with some dire penalty and then if he persisted, as he generally did, carried it out. Butch, our housemaster, showed none of their decisiveness when he was confronted with the problem. One famous evening he appeared in our bedroom to put out the light as usual. He growled goodnight to us, but instead of closing the door on our muttered replies, he heard one of Duffer's ripest eruptions. He stood for a moment, his hand frozen above the light-switch, his face a picture of stunned disbelief, and then took the better part of valour by retreating abruptly. The bedroom monitor had the greatest difficulty in quietening our laughter, and Duffer's happy accident, as it seemed then, went unpunished. He bided his time.

On his nightly rounds, Butch would sometimes attempt to engage us in conversation, though our churlishness and his awkwardness usually ensured that these chats were lamely one-sided, leaving him with no choice except to withdraw in despair. But an evening came when he decided to be more energetic in his campaign to teach us the civilized art. Somewhat self-consciously, he took up his position in the middle of the room and launched a formal topic for discussion – capital punishment, or the virtues of idealism over pragmatism perhaps. He made a short speech, airing the pros and cons, and then waited for our response. None came.

'Well, gentlemen,' he rumbled convivially, 'have you no opinions of your own?'

This was Duffer's moment, and he took it. The fart rolled sonorously from his bed; a basso profundo fart which was as deep as it was loud. Duffer raised his bedclothes for added acoustical effect.

Thunderstruck – almost literally – Butch could only gasp, 'I beg your pardon?'

Duffer's brass spoke again, still more fruitily.

'Are you ill, McDuff? Do you want to excuse yourself?'

'No, sir.' Another mighty blast. 'Sorry, sir. Can't help it.'

'Go to the lavatory,' Butch bellowed at him. 'And see matron in the morning.'

The next day Duffer was given a monstrous charcoal sandwich to eat, which was clearly designed more to punish than to cure. That night we all lay in our beds, shivering with anticipation. In spite of a terrible warning issued by the bedroom monitor, Duffer could not let the opportunity pass. Though Butch did no more than put his head round the door, not daring to risk another incident, he was too slow. Duffer caught him, this time with a fart as sharp as a sniper's bullet. Badly winged, Butch shut the door and crept away.

What could the poor man do? Typically, he chose not to see that Duffer was being provocative, and took the only other course open to him. McDuff, he announced, was the victim of chronic flatulence and must be treated accordingly. The matron was instructed to put him on a special diet, and when that proved ineffective, the doctor was summoned. He prescribed a variety of repulsive-looking absorbents, all of which Duffer willingly swallowed, but these too produced no result and in the end there was talk of sending him to hospital for tests.

Meanwhile, Duffer himself revelled in his unsavoury fame; he also refined his control and timbre to the point of artistry, making himself a positive Petomane. But as the term wore on, his talent lost its power to shock and amuse and became a bore. For a while, it seemed as if he had become addicted to his now unwelcome trick, which he performed continually and without any regard for his public's growing disgust. Fortunately for him, the holidays intervened and when he returned the following term, though he could not resist giving us an occasional reminder of his curious skill, he devoted himself for the most part to finding other means of bedevilling the authorities and entertaining the rest of us.

For all his stupidity, I liked Duffer, as did Tom, and the three of us spent many a happy Saturday afternoon together, wandering through the town or fooling about in the house. At the same time, I knew that I had a vested interest in his playing the clown of our generation: as long as he was conspicuous, I could pass unnoticed and therefore evade being teased. Duffer would probably have been much the way he was even if his accent had not been ridiculed, for long after people had ceased to notice it he continued to court trouble. The wretched Bones was another matter. I dread to think of the damage done to him at school. Perhaps he shrugged it off; perhaps he took no scars away with him; perhaps he was thick-skinned and resilient. Perhaps – but I doubt it. At all events, the treatment meted out to him, the Scratcher and others made a terrible impression on me in my first term, and I swore I would never become the butt of anyone's teasing.

Looking back on my thirteen-year-old self, I cannot see that I was any less laughable than those around me, but somehow I did manage to avoid getting laughed at on a regular basis. I was certainly fortunate in having a plain name with no obvious invitations to satire – unlike Poole, for example, who was ineluctably dubbed 'Tool'. For a brief spell at prep school I had gone by the feeble sobriquet of 'Harry', but it had not stuck, and at Shrewsbury I was never called anything except my unadulterated surname until my friends and I reached the age when we began, shyly, to use our Christian names. A plain name in itself of course was no guarantee of safety, and I can only attribute my escape to sheer luck and a dash of astute ingratiation. Making oneself agreeable had to be undertaken judiciously, because nothing was more likely to backfire than an effort to please which was interpreted as 'oiliness' or 'groising'.

In seeking a smooth passage through school I had two advantages, the first being that I had no desire to buck the system; on the contrary, I liked it, and conforming to its many

oddities, if not always a pleasure, did make for a fulfilled life.
Having endured the austerity of my prep school for four years,
I quickly learnt to relish the intricacies and absurdities of this
new regime. I came to enjoy its elaborate scheme of privileges,
its arcane rules (I passed my colour test with no difficulty), its
special vocabulary and personality cults. Later, I became very
impatient with all this rigmarole, but at the beginning, once I
had got the hang of it, I found the very complexity of the
system a source of security. I saw too that it could be made to
work both ways – for you as well as against – and that its
cumbersome ramifications left plenty of room for small,
private deviations.

My second advantage was that I was able to make close
friends, and these friendships rendered the place not merely
tolerable, but exceedingly enjoyable. If this was a virtue, it was
one born as much out of necessity as out of any natural
aptitude. Around the time I was sent away to prep school a
series of unfortunate coincidences resulted in my losing every
one of the little circle of friends I had belonged to at home in
Aigburth. Leonore, Anthony and Brian, or rather their
parents, all moved away from Liverpool during that year, an
accident which made my sense of expulsion all the more
complete. My parents also suffered from the departure of these
families, though my mother probably felt their loss more
keenly than my father, for whom this was a period of great
activity and fulfilment. Not only was he making a success of
his legal practice, an achievement which brought him the
deepest satisfaction, but he was also taking part in local
Conservative politics at night. His motives were as much
professional as political: although he has been a life-long
Conservative voter, and at that time may even have been
ambitious for office, he believed, quite rightly as it turned out,
that he would be able to attract clients through the party. He
was hardly the first to make such a calculation; nonetheless, he
was punctilious in his attendance at meetings and zealous in

his canvassing during elections, and for a while he found the political life exhilarating. My mother, also a Conservative voter, kept aloof from his politics, confining her involvement to the many dinner-dances that seemed to be an essential feature of municipal Conservatism in those days.

When not working on behalf of the party, my father devoted his evenings to writing the first of his books. All his life he has had a powerful but unfocused creative urge, which has impelled him to take up an enormous variety of what must, I suppose, be called hobbies. He has turned his hand to carving, clay-modelling, photography, painting, drawing and cartoon-ing – his favourite – and has disgraced himself in none of them. His writing was like his politics in being ambivalently inspired: he set out to write a law book with a view to enhancing his professional reputation as well as for the sake of its intrinsic rewards. The book itself, *Advocacy At Petty Sessions* (a guide for barristers, solicitors, police officers and others who appear as advocates before magistrates' courts) was written during my first years at prep school and published in 1956.

He discovered that the process of writing was for him, as it is for me, physically laborious and mentally painful, and he claimed that he could only concentrate in my mother's presence. He had no study or room of his own in those days, so he sat at a desk in the sitting-room, with books heaped up at his elbows and round his feet, covering sheet after sheet of thick blue foolscap with his sloped handwriting (on which I later modelled my own) while my mother was required to sit reading or knitting in silence.

The book cost him a great deal of effort over many hours, and my mother was therefore called on to play his muse for the great majority of the evenings he was at home. There was no risk of these evenings being interrupted because neither of my parents, but especially not my mother, relished or encouraged spontaneous visits to the house. Once the Franklands had left the district, they put their social life on a strictly formal basis, issuing their rare invitations well in advance so as to leave my mother plenty of time to bring her preparations to the necessary state of perfection. As a result, their diminished circle of friends remained as it was, and if they did meet new people with children my age I never got to see them often enough to replace my lost gang.

We became an exclusive and reclusive family. I do not remember anyone coming to stay except my grandparents from Pembroke, who paid very infrequent visits. While I was at home during the holidays, my mother deliberately refrained from inviting people to the house, feeling that she should devote herself exclusively to me. Thus, people did not come for lunch, or drop in for drinks, and though there must have been some dinner parties, they would have taken place in the ceremonial grandeur of our dining-room at an hour long after my rigidly enforced bedtime. My father entertained his clients at lunch in the city, and did not bring his political pals home. My mother went to coffee mornings, sherry parties and bridge afternoons, but she probably saw more of my grandmother – her mother-in-law – with whom she went shopping, than anyone else.

During these years I was perforce a solitary child, though I cannot say I felt lonely. I developed an emotional and creative self-sufficiency which has stood me in good stead as a writer though, ironically, it separated me from my parents. As my internal world grew richer, so it grew more private and discrete. At first, my solitariness did not affect me, or even strike me as such, for I was glad simply to be at home and not at school. I dreaded the end of the holidays, counting off the days like a prisoner on release. But as the years went by, and particularly once I was at Shrewsbury, I found myself looking forward with keener and keener anticipation to the start of each term when I would be reunited with my friends. Then I counted the days with barely containable excitement, willing the last week to pass as quickly as I had willed the last week of term at my prep school to pass.

Within a few days of arriving at Shrewsbury I befriended a fellow new scum. He was called Thompson, and was a studious, earnest boy with an elder brother in the house who was known as 'Buttocks'. United mostly by our need for mutual protection, Thompson II and I soon got into the habit of going everywhere and doing everything together. Every morning we walked together from the house to the chapel, a journey of a quarter of a mile, and at the end of the day's lessons we waited for each other outside the school buildings to walk back to the house. We spent our half-days together, we watched cricket matches and rowing races together, we went into town together, and whenever possible we sat next to each other.

We never discussed or made explicit the terms of our friendship, but we certainly expected fidelity from each other and it was unfailingly given throughout that first summer term. For my part, I also expected a certain intimacy from my friend, or at least a willingness to soak up my garrulous confidences, and Thompson II, though not much given to autobiography himself, was always content to listen to my gossip and anxieties. However, when my old friend Tom came from our prep school to Shrewsbury the following term, I am sorry to confess that I dropped Thompson II and hardly ever spoke to him again during the entire remainder of our time at school.

Tom and I immediately formed the same sort of exclusive partnership, except that Tom was no less loquacious and confiding than I. Furthermore, he was blessed, as Thompson II was not, with an expansive sense of humour; he was not only funny himself, but quick to appreciate another's joke, and quicker still to see the ridiculous in others, at which he would laugh freely and infectiously. It is a curious fact that most people are incapable of true laughter; when amused, they cough, snort, bellow, snicker, wheeze or squeak (I am of the bellowing and squeaking breed), they grunt and honk, they release falsetto noises from somewhere between their ears, they hiss like snakes, they give silent imitations of mirthfulness or shout out 'ha ha' as if taking laughing lessons; they make a hundred different sounds which pass for laughter but are not the real thing. Tom was one of those rare beings who could throw back his head, open his mouth and let loose a glorious, musical flow of sheer joyfulness, and once that mellow sound began to bubble out of him it was impossible, no matter how dire the consequences might be, not to laugh with him.

During our first few terms Tom and I were inseparable; indeed, our friendship was sometimes commented on, though more in a spirit of interest than mockery. We may even have been envied by boys for whom the difficulties of school life were made all the harder to bear by loneliness. At all events, we were never teased with real venom; nor was it suggested that our closeness was 'queer'. Anyone making such a suggestion would have done so at his peril, for Tom possessed a fearsome temper. He was strong for his age and when roused was recklessly pugnacious.

Ours may have been unusually intimate, but the development of special friendships was a natural response to the highly unnatural circumstances in which we had all been brought up since the age of eight or so. They were the only available substitute for the relationships that had been cut short, starved or forgotten as a result of our being sent to school. Without either side being more than vaguely aware of it, friends were required to compensate for the absence of parents, brothers and sisters, grandparents, aunts, uncles and the friends who had been left behind. We were deprived of the important and casual figures who make up the ordinary social life of an adolescent living at home. We had no contact with older people who were not members of staff, with younger children who were not automatically inferior, with older boys who did not enjoy some form of power over us, or with boys of our age from other schools. We had no contact, in other words, with anyone who was not in some way implicated in the school's regime and therefore set at a distance. And all this is to say nothing of the gravest omission of the lot: girls. Any girl whom we encountered on the site – and they were a very rare phenomenon – was by definition taboo, for she was either a maid or a master's daughter. Both species, whether they liked it or not, were protected from us by the most stringent laws. Thus the medium of friendship was asked to carry a very tangled freight of emotions, a function complicated by the fact that many of us were blind to our own situation.

I must not exaggerate. Some boys were able to suspend their emotional needs for the duration of the term, picking up where they had left off at the end of the last holiday. Some boys were emotionally so sluggish that they made no effort to console themselves for the loss of their home circle, and some had become so numbed by their repeated absences from home that they no longer felt their loss. Or so it appeared. But maybe they were too proud to admit to their needs, or too cold to express them, or too cautious to show them. There was no way of telling, and at that age we lacked the acuity to guess and – it must be said – the charity to care. The lonely were left to their loneliness, the friendless were not befriended and the unhappy went uncomforted. Very few boys broke under the strain, but for many the price of adapting to this emotional solitary confinement was that their capacity to feel was either iced over or submerged so deep it could never be brought to the surface again. Tom and I were among the lucky ones who were not forced to suppress or fear their feelings.

In adolescence, friendship between people of the same sex can act as a sort of rehearsal for marriage – albeit an unwitting one, a safe experiment which permits a similar intimacy, as well as the same day-by-day familiarity, but makes no demands in the way of sex, money, children and all the other potential irritants of an adult alliance. At the same time, friendship is the great alternative to the family; it provides neutral territory where for the first time people can form relationships on their own initiative and on their own terms. In the case of those for whom home life was in some way deficient (Tom's father had died when he was no more than a baby, and another of my close friends had been put through the mincing machine of a recriminative divorce), friendship proved to be far more than an expedient resort, a mere port in the storm of school life; it proved to be a very rich communion – much richer, it seemed, than the old bond tying us to our parents.

I do not want to make false claims for Tom and myself. For a while we were very close, but we did not represent ideal comradeship, or anything like it. True, we were both emotionally highly charged and brought to all our relationships an occasional extreme of intensity; on the other hand, he was too mischievous, I was too light-hearted and we were both too gregarious to allow our friendship to become unhealthily introverted.

Later, he terrified me with his daring, for like McDuff he soon graduated from mere mischief to serious delinquency, though unlike McDuff he was too intelligent to make an exhibition of it. Tom was a rebel on a far more serious – and dangerous – scale, and it was not just school, but society itself that he was preparing to fight. Like quite a few boys of our generation, he rejected his middle-class background, allying himself instead with the working class, or rather with a sort of machismo-masochistic version of it which was part Orwellian in its thirst for degradation and part James Dean in its glorification of the inarticulate prole. The working-class way of life, he told me angrily, was far more 'real' than ours, which was soft and false. This realism was distinguished by sweat, muscle, manual work, jeans, and money earned with your own labour, not someone else's. He sneered at me as a typical product of my class, an effete ponce who would not last ten minutes on a building site. (That much was certainly true.)

His identification with the workers did not bring him to politics, and I suspect he would have been furious had anyone accused him of being a socialist or a 'bolshie', to use the vernacular. As it happened, nobody did, because we were politically a very ignorant lot. If anything, Tom was an authoritarian going through an inverted phase, which caused him to side with the victims rather than the rulers, without prompting him to question the system that made them victims. But then his adoption of working-class ways, as he understood them, was more emotional than rational, giving him the chance to vent his considerable aggression. At all events, what his new identity amounted to was a longing to get out of school and do some real work (he did in time get to dig up the streets of Manchester), and a taste in the meantime for T-shirts, jeans, bristling short haircuts and a fiercely challenging way of speaking.

It also entailed the ownership of a motorbike. Not for Tom the odd pint of illicit beer or a furtive visit to the 'flicks'; he was only satisfied with a truly criminal piece of rebellion. Simply to sit on a motorbike, never mind ride on one, was an offence punishable with expulsion; to own a motorbike was a short cut to the electric chair. I have no idea what its make or power was; I only know that it was a huge, gleaming, metallic beast which Tom kept in a barn, and that I was terrified of it. On Sunday afternoons and half-holidays he would take me on its back, and I don't know whether I was more frightened of the machine, which was far friskier than any horse I had ever ridden, or of Tom cursing me in front for being a coward. Fortunately, he was not much of a mechanic, a power freak rather than a genuine bike freak, and when its engine failed for some reason, he did not try to mend it, or learn how; he simply sold it and turned to a fresh source of mayhem.

But all this came later. In our first few terms our amusements were more innocent, or at least more law-abiding, and involved nothing more serious than contriving new ways of landing poor Duffer in trouble. As the terms rolled by, our need for protective exclusivity wore off, and though our friendship kept its primacy (we took to staying at each other's homes during the holidays) we began to enter into the most sociable and carefree phase of our school careers. We both relished the moments when small knots of us would gather in the corridors to gossip and deride our elders and inferiors, or in the library to swap 'feelthy' stories, for which I had no memory or talent for telling, or in the recreation room to shout and laugh over the snooker table. In the evenings after prep, we would collect in a study with a working gramophone and listen to new records bought in the holidays or old favourites. I remember being especially fond of Lonnie Donegan, a skiffle group called the Vipers, Eartha Kitt (then at her greatest), the Everly Brothers, Buddy Holly and, of course, Elvis. These were the years of the King's impressment in the Army, but we were only just catching up with his earliest – and best – songs. If they were fast, we danced to them with frantic muscularity, and if they were slow, we listened with sneering cynicism and a secret lump in our throats. 'Are You Lonesome Tonight?' with its laughable reference to Shakespeare – 'someone said, "the world's a stage"' – was extremely popular. Sometimes we listened for the thousandth time to *At The Drop of a Hat* or *Beyond the Fringe*, never failing to collapse in helpless group hysteria at the best bits – Alan Bennett's sermon – 'And Esau was an hairy man' – for instance, or Peter Cook's call for volunteers: 'We need a futile gesture, Smithers.' On Sundays we never missed 'Round the Horn', greeting every hoary catch-phrase with horse laughs. 'The answer loies in the soil,' we would chorus, blithely echoing Kenneth Williams week after week, and then repeating ourselves mirthfully throughout the rest of the day.

These were frequent but intensely happy moments during which I would be overcome with a sense of mutual hilarity and benevolence. Such moments are not a common feature of adult life.

NINE

During holidays I was, as I have said, a solitary, though not lonely child. I also led what might be considered a boring life, though I was in fact seldom bored. It was a life not much interrupted by visitors or friends, in which both sets of grandparents continued to play an important – perhaps too important – part.

From my early childhood I have no memories of my Liverpool grandparents to compare with those of my farming grandparents, and until my fourteenth or fifteenth year my father's father the judge remained a shadowy and somewhat awesome figure, an august personage more often referred to than actually seen. I don't think I stayed overnight at their flat very often – maybe only once – but I do recall lying in bed as a small boy in their tiny spare room, too shy to get out, and listening to my grandfather going about his morning routine. Wherever he went and whatever he did, he accompanied himself with a tuneless whistle; it was a whistle that had no pretensions to music at all, but was simply a noise made out of habit to confirm his existence in the silence of the morning. His whistle was drowned for a moment by the rattling of the grate and then reasserted itself as he carried last night's ash and clinkers out to the dustbin at the back door. I caught a glimpse of him passing my door, a ludicrous figure, though not so to my childish eye, in his camel-hair dressing gown and bowler hat. He invariably wore a hat to perform this chore for fear that the ash would get into his hair, about which he was extremely self-conscious. He kept it cut militarily short, visiting his barber once a week to ensure that his steeply pitched skull was shorn to the skin except at the very apex. Each morning he carefully massaged his scalp with bay rum, whose spicy aroma made a nauseating concoction when mixed with the biting smell of mothballs, in which all his clothes were heavily steeped. Still lying in bed, I heard the fierce hiss of his brush and comb as he fought to flatten his bristly tuft of hair. Despite his precautions, a small whorl of hair growing from his double crown always managed to spring free and stand incorrigibly above the rest, a little sprig of nature stubbornly defying every effort of artifice.

I have much sharper childhood memories of Granny, so called to distinguish her from Grandma in Stackpole. Her name was Betty, but she was never called anything other than Queenie, which suggested the amateurish monarch of a tin-pot kingdom and suited her perfectly. Although she was dainty, elegant and chic, there was nevertheless something earthy about her, something beneath the silk and make-up that hinted of life's coarser side. She had a lively sense of the absurd,

especially her husband's absurdities, and her irrepressible
flippancy made a pleasant contrast to his tendency to pomp
and self-importance. The contrast of her often vulgar tongue
with her regal appearance was amusing too, and rendered her
very approachable to a child.

Her emotions were probably shallower than his, more self-
centred and calculating, but she was also much less demanding. If the world was right with her, and it mostly was, then she
was content to leave others to their own devices. I do not think
she brooded over me or hatched grandiose plans for my
adulthood. She quite rightly assumed that our relationship
would be satisfactory to both parties if she confined her role to
giving me, her only grandchild, a regular quota of treats.
Having spent much of her own life contriving to lay on treats
for herself, she understood their secret, which is that they
should never be scanted.

And so, as soon as I was old enough to enjoy it, she arranged
to take me out on my own for a day in Liverpool at the
beginning and end of each school holiday. Making an 'early
start' (around eleven o'clock), we strolled from the flat to the
main road in search of a taxi. Rain or shine, her mere
appearance at the curb was enough to bring a cab hurtling to
our service. Once we were on our way, a time-honoured ritual
took place. Producing a ten-shilling note from her wafer-thin
handbag, she would ask me if I had any change to give the
driver as a tip, and with a splendid disdain for equity exchange
my florin or shilling for her note.

The driver was instructed to drop us at the bottom of Bold
Street, then the Bond Street of Liverpool, where we proceeded
to do what she was pleased to call her shopping. She must have
had food and other household necessities delivered to the flat,
because I never knew her to buy anything of the slightest
domestic usefulness. She changed her book at Boots' subscrip-
tion library, she toyed with a pair of gloves at Cripps, tried on a
hat at George Henry Lee, bought a quarter of Turkish delight

at Coopers, and then, thoroughly exhausted, hailed another cab to take us to Sissons for lunch.

It was not what she bought or where she went that I relished so much as her manner of doing it, for like her husband she was nothing if not stylish. She had a way of giving the impression that she was a person of tremendous importance. Her manner was not grand, and certainly not overbearing, but she had a dignified frailty which prompted the world to leap to her assistance. In her company, the simple business of getting about was turned into a pageant. We did not walk down the street like other beings, we processed arm in arm, she picking her way along the imaginary red carpet that seemed to unroll before her, I carrying her preposterously small parcels. We did not just go into a shop, ordinary customers with ordinary money to spend; we somehow contrived to make a flamboyant entrance as if we were dignitaries come to cut a tape and open the place to the public.

Sissons, where we invariably had our lunch, boasted a certain grandeur from the outside, for its doorway was flanked by a pair of massive marble pillars which were mottled in bruised shades of purple and brown. Inside, it proved to be more modest, but it was nonetheless exceedingly respectable, catering for ladies who, like my grandmother, wore not only hats but veils too. Here I had been brought as a small child in velvet knickerbockers to have tea. My mother, who saw disease crawling from every pore of Liverpool's skin, used to insist that my food was served in a silver porringer which she brought in her handbag for the purpose. This little bowl, which was a christening present, had four handles made in the shape of half moons with faces cut into them, and I kept it until it was stolen, many years later, from my London flat.

Once we were inside Sissons, the best part of my special day began. Over lunch we studied the cinema listings in the *Echo*. Going to the pictures, as my grandmother called it, was as much of a treat for her as it was for me. In those days Liverpool was rich in cinemas, and Lime Street was virtually lined with them. My favourite, as a building, was the lushly named Palais de Luxe, which had over its marquee a bas-relief statue of a projectionist hunched in thrilling concentration over his projector.

After the most careful deliberation, we selected our film, paid the bill and summoned a further taxi. Although her taste in most things was unswervingly bourgeois, and although she very seldom strayed from Liverpool's smaller equivalent of the West End, on these occasions she threw respectability to the winds and went wherever our choice of film dictated. Ticket-sellers in their remote kiosks, used only to old-age pensioners seeking warmth and forlorn schoolboys trying to con their way into X-certificate pictures, were amazed to see this incongruous, over-dressed pair standing at the window de-manding tickets for the balcony.

Of the many films we saw together, I can remember only one with any clarity, and that was *The Hunchback of Notre Dame*, on account of the incomparably voluptuous Gina Lollobrig-ida. I sometimes wonder what influence, if any, Queenie herself had on my subsequent taste in women. She represented a type of femininity which is very unfashionable today, for she never earned a penny all her life and would have thought it the greatest folly to exchange her silken chains for liberation. Though she was utterly reliant on the judge for her every material need, he was in truth her slave, and liked nothing more than to be the victim of her winsome extortions. With her platinum-blonde hair and china-doll features, her cock-tails and diamonds, her hats and furs, she was, I suppose, a cliché of her time and class, but she added a dash of shrewd vulgarity all her own which if it did not make her altogether lovable, certainly made her popular.

Like her husband, Queenie was an incorrigible smoker, and in due course she suffered a fatal thrombosis, thought to have been induced by cigarettes (du Mauriers, actually). She did not die at once but lay, slowly weakening and mostly unconscious, in a nursing home, where my grandfather and my father visited her every day. Then one morning, she surprised the nurses by rallying and demanding that she should look her best for the judge's visit that afternoon. Her hair was done, her make-up put on for the first time in a week, and she was propped up in bed wearing her pearls and a new bed-jacket to receive him. When he came, she held his hand, told him she loved him, and died.

I was at school when it happened. My mother wrote first to say she was ill. I bought her a couple of jigsaws, her favourite amusement after patience, and sent them to the nursing home. The parcel was opened for her, and I am told she knew what the presents were and who had sent them. My mother wrote again, telling me she had died. At my grandfather's insistence, I was not brought back to Liverpool for the funeral. His life was destroyed by her death, and he wanted to grieve alone and unwatched; if he had had his way, he would have been her only mourner at the cremation.

As for myself, I do not remember feeling anything stronger than a brief spasm of sadness. But then, my treats notwithstanding, I had never been close to her, and my loss did not seem great. On the other hand, I am now convinced that I should have attended her funeral. It is not easy for children, and perhaps still less so for adolescents, to grasp the nature of certain adult emotions, and I certainly had no idea at the time how deeply my grandfather was wounded by her death, nor how painfully he suffered in the years that followed. Had I been to the funeral and seen his grief, I might have understood his feelings better and behaved differently towards him in his wretched loneliness. As it was, I never saw him cry, I never heard him mention her grievingly, I never even saw him upset; or if I did I either turned away in embarrassment or did not recognize his feelings for what they were. My father must have suffered, too, but I never saw him show his feelings; he certainly never discussed them with me. Nor did my mother, who had been very close to Queenie.

I am not saying that my going to her funeral would have changed anything in itself – after all, if my grandfather had been the kind of person to show and share his feelings, the funeral would never have been an issue – but Queenie's death was yet another event attached to my home life from which I was separated by being at school. It served to reinforce my sense of being a stranger in both my spheres of existence. By the time I returned home it had become a part of history, an experience which had been discussed, coped with and digested; but it was not part of my history, because I had gone through none of these processes.

My two lives now hardly interpenetrated. The holidays were reduced to a limbo where I simply waited for them to finish, suspended in a not unpleasant state of emptiness. I no longer properly belonged in my own home. It had become a place I visited regularly, where I was made welcome and felt content, but from whose internal, emotional life I was excluded. Nor did I belong in school, which in spite of my friends could never be an alternative to home. In so far as I belonged anywhere, it was in an abstract, floating world of my own making, which I carried about with me like a lunatic with his carrier bags. This world teemed with real and imaginary people, with icons and ogres, and was flexibly located in familiar landscapes and dream countries. It was shortly to be peopled still more richly with mythical figures from history who were to come to seem far more real to me, and to impinge far more decisively on my thinking, than any of the shadowy adults at Shrewsbury or even my parents.

The immediate result of my grandmother's death was that the judge sold his flat and moved into a hotel almost opposite as a resident. Though he soon learnt to treat the lounge, hall, reading-room and other public rooms as if they were part of his house which he had graciously agreed to share with others, he arranged to have his bedroom furnished with his own bed, bookcase, table and chair and a few treasures from his old home. The rest of the flat's furniture was disposed of, and some of it found its way into our house. The desk my father had been using was replaced by a much grander affair, a stately, polished edifice of mahogany whose lid yawned open to expose a red leather tongue and a multitude of little brass and ivory fillings. His old desk was taken up to my room, which began to be transformed from a playroom into something more like a study, though long after I had left home and married it was still referred to as 'the nursery'. A custom-made bookcase was installed, and one of the cowhide armchairs was brought up from the sitting-room, which had entered yet another phase in my mother's scheme for gentrifying our little villa. I had always been used to spending long hours in my room, and now that it was converted into a flatteringly grown-up environment I retreated into it still more often. During the course of my lengthy occupation, this room had many identities thrust on to it, most of them deriving from books, and with the arrival of my leather chair it acquired the air of Bulldog Drummond's club, the headquarters where he plotted the downfall of his evil adversary, Carl Peterson. However, I only had to stand up and make for the window to find myself pacing the quarterdeck of a lurching frigate under full sail as I adopted the uniform and quiet heroism of Captain Hornblower. Some years before, I had requested a gramophone for Christmas and when it arrived, a splendid Grundig in red-and-cream leatherette capable of carrying six records on its automatic spindle, I remember wondering what to buy to play on it. The only record I had then heard of, though not actually heard (I was still at prep school) was *High Society*, which I duly went out and purchased. It was a happy choice. By the time my room was revamped my taste had of course changed and so, somewhat anachronistically, Hornblower was in the habit of scanning the horizon for Frenchies to the strains of Duane Eddy, Johnny Ray and Frankie Lane.

Most days I spent at least an hour mindlessly knocking a tennis ball against the kitchen wall, or playing interminable games of Jokari, at which I became rather expert, or playing fives in the improvised court made by our back door and coal bunkers. Sometimes I was dispatched to Booker Avenue on shopping expeditions and every evening I helped my father with the washing up, but otherwise I contributed nothing to the running of the house; nor did my parents ask me to. My holiday world contracted to the confines of my room; but this was no prison, for it became instead a basket in which I sailed across a different, imaginary world, suspended from a balloon of fantasy.

In describing my lugubrious holidays, I must not be unfair to my mother. Though in her own reclusiveness she did not relieve my isolation, she did everything she could to make my life at home agreeable and was herself unfailingly good company. We talked easily and still do. However, by the time I was fourteen I had outgrown the desire to confide, and was willing to bring only my material needs within her sphere of aid. At her insistence, I was kept in the lap of modest luxury, and in order to minister to me she delayed her business début until my first year at university, when she opened her dress shop and made a stylish success of it. While I was at home, she always left me to my own devices, and this was much more positive than neglectful; she tolerated my whims and never queried my tastes and interests; she trusted my judgement, she loyally supported all my efforts and unreservedly applauded my small achievements. Nor has she changed since those days.

I also must not leave an impression of my mother as a household drudge. True, my father made it a point of principle that he, as the breadwinner, could not be expected to do any chores, and apart from his admittedly strenuous exertions in the garden he did not lift a hand. He was, for example, used to leaving his clothes on the floor for someone else to pick up and wash. But this someone else was not usually my mother. It was her daily help, who did indeed come daily and worked all morning. Her name was Mrs Dobson, though she was known to all of us as 'Dobbie'. My mother, when talking to her about my father, referred to him as 'the Master', and hoped she would do the same. Dobbie was always kind and friendly to me, but we never really talked to each other. Our relationship was yet another aspect of my peculiar state of dissociation in my own home: here was this nice woman rattling around our house (and it was a small house) every weekday morning, who had known me since I was a small boy but was nonetheless a virtual stranger to me.

To get out of the house, I sometimes took my roller-skates to the promenade or walked the dog down there. Sometimes my mother took me on shopping expeditions to Liverpool and we would meet Queenie at Fullers for lunch. I would be taken to Watson and Prickards to buy shoes or a tweed jacket and have my hair cut by the Pole in the basement who also cut my father's and my grandfather's hair. And afterwards I would be taken to Thomas Youngs, the booksellers, where my mother and grandmother would occasionally shake their heads over my choices. On the whole my taste was conventional enough: Biggles, Bunter, Bulldog Drummond, Sherlock Holmes, Professor Challenger, the novels of Rider Haggard and Robert Louis Stevenson and so on – nothing, in short, that was not at least twenty years old, and most of it far older.

Sometimes my mother took me further afield to visit the last of her aunts, who lived in Bowdon, Cheshire. Aunty Maud, the youngest sister of my mother's mother, was a hugely fat woman with a head of pure white hair that had once been red, a pair of petulant lips and a luminously florid complexion. Before each meal she would self-righteously consume an Energen roll designed for people trying to lose weight, then with a clear conscience she would tuck into the gargantuan platefuls that explained her gross size. She had no children of her own and did not really know how to treat me. As a small boy I was frightened of her loud voice and aggressive manner which, looking back, I think she intended to be jocular. On one occasion she truly terrified me. Climbing the stairs of her house, I reached the point where I could see the length of her narrow landing, at the end of which was a small lavatory. There sat my aunt, having left the door wide open. As I stared at the nightmare of bulging thighs, straining suspenders and dropped knickers, she did not close the door, but gaily called out to me, 'It's all right. I expect you've seen it all before.'

I had never seen any such thing before, and never wanted to again. I fled.

We began to vary our family holidays in Stackpole with trips elsewhere. I was shown the sights in London and later those in Paris, which most memorably included naked girls in the Folies Bergères suspended from the ceiling on a huge wheel to form a human chandelier. That evening I drank copious amounts of Chianti in defiance of my parents' anxious warnings and was royally sick in the night. By then we had also had our first summer holiday abroad, in Belgium, and had become devotees of Portmeirion Hotel, that pleasure dome in Wales which has since tragically burnt down. My parents encouraged me to bring friends with us both to Stackpole and Portmeirion, and this I did, though they were of course drawn from school rather than Liverpool.

As I grew older, I started to visit Liverpool on my own, spending whole days doing little more than walking its streets and haunting its public buildings – the Walker Art Gallery and the museum next door; Lime Street Station, where for some reason I passed many mesmerizing hours simply watching the passengers milling around and the steam trains pulling in and out; St John's Market (now demolished); the second-hand bookshops in the shabby district at the back of Bold Street; the Cathedral (the Anglican rather than the Catholic one, which had yet to be built); and of course the Pierhead (now abominably redesigned) to watch the ships and liners that still used the docks in those days or catch the ferry to Birkenhead for the sheer pleasure of looking back on the doomed grandeur of Liverpool's waterfront.

Sometimes I called at my father's cluttered, dusty office in Dale Street, where I was fussed over by his secretary Dot, for whom I conceived a maudlin infatuation. If he had time, he would take me to the Kardomah, the gossip shop of the city's legal community, and buy me coffee or lunch. I felt proud of him then, seeing him so full of bustle and confidence. He seemed to be at home in these sooty, pompous streets; he knew how the city worked; he knew who everybody was, and he had a joke for each person we met. He would introduce me to his friends, and out of respect for him they would be polite to me and ask when I was going to join the family firm.

Unfortunately, it was at about this time – I was perhaps fifteen – that I first experienced twinges of ambivalence in my feelings for my father. Hitherto he had been a warm and heroic if distant figure, whose quips and stories had always amused me. After my voice had broken, people often mistook me for him when I answered the telephone, and this pleased me enormously. I was still more pleased when I was told, as I sometimes was, that I had acquired my father's gift for telling comic anecdotes, and I consciously imitated his style of spinning out a trivial incident until it attained the stature of a mock epic. The sound of laughter had become very sweet to me at school, for I had discovered the well-known fact that making others laugh was a way of disarming them, or at least of deflecting their hostility. Laughter is a kind of love, too, and I had learnt to crave its intoxicating warmth. I discovered that I had a flair for the spontaneous wisecrack, but I also took care to work up my facility for the prolonged, set-piece story told in my father's manner. It was pleasant to be able to close the gap between home and school, and bring him into my study for a moment by echoing his style and using some of his special words.

I was therefore more than a little disconcerted to find myself becoming the butt of his jokes, losing my old position as his sidekick and ever-appreciative audience. At first I did not wholly resent the change; indeed, for a while I laughed as heartily as he over his jokes at my expense. I had assimilated his sense of humour so thoroughly that even when I became its target I shared quite genuinely in his derision. Soon enough, however, my amusement turned to discomfort and, as his teasing grew habitual, to misery. Despite all the trouble I had gone to at school to protect myself against 'rotting', here I was at home, where I had assumed I was most safe, being attacked by someone who left me helpless with gibes to which I had no reply except a wan smile. And by appearing to take his teasing in good part, I only encouraged him.

The immediate object of his mockery was my nose, which might have been thought to have suffered enough indignities already. As puberty wreaked its havoc on my limbs and organs, I suddenly acquired my present stature of six feet, and overnight my nose ballooned into its imposing adult proportions, leaving the rest of my face still in a state of moderate boyhood. At a stroke, or so it seemed, I was transmuted into a pubescent de Gaulle: I was all height and hooter. I was also taller now than my father, though this seemed to confer no advantage. His jokes were not subtle or original. He would cheerily inform my mother that my 'conk' had arrived in the room a good five minutes before me, and she, perhaps provocatively, always insisted on my immaculate good looks. How on earth, he wondered, did I manage to get about without overbalancing? They would have to buy a bigger car to make room for my conk. And so on. It did not take him long to get into the habit of calling me 'Big Conk'. He could not possibly have known the pain he was causing me because pride and confusion led me to keep up an enigmatic front, smiling thinly but never protesting, which he presumably interpreted as evidence of my ability to take a joke. It never occurred to me to ask him to stop, or to ask my mother to intervene, far less to make references to his own not inconsiderable nose from which my own was, after all, directly descended. The awful thing was that I thought his mockery was probably justified. Where there was a clumsy malice, I saw only jocularity. His authority over me was then far too powerful for me even to think of questioning his right to tease, and I could not reconcile the hurt I felt with the fact that this was my father, whose most lovable, entertaining quality was his partiality for jokes. A double bind, if ever there was one.

His mockery of my nose only endorsed my own worst suspicions, for like most adolescents I was becoming exceedingly sensitive about my appearance, and was convinced that I was growing into a virtual freak. I believed not only that my nose was grotesquely enlarged, but also that my chin was pitifully small. As a result, I spent many uncomfortable hours thrusting the latter out, locking my teeth in a prognathic jut worthy of a Habsburg in the hope that my whole face would restructure itself. None of my features satisfied me. I had dark curly hair, so naturally I pined for straight fair hair. I am full-lipped, with green eyes and a high complexion, so I yearned for the opposite, searching hour by hour in the triple mirror in our bathroom for evidence that I was turning into a Viking – thin-lipped, blue-eyed, pale and chiselled. I was lucky to escape the adolescent's cruellest plague, acne, but my relative freedom from spots brought me no comfort. My longing for a face other than my own, other than the one my father was – understandably – satirizing, grew steadily more intense.

For the first time in my life I was conscious of being subjected to my father's disapproval, or at least of his having mixed feelings for me. Up until now, it had never occurred to me to question my parents' attitude one way or the other; I had assumed that they never looked other than favourably on me and all my doings. I received a considerable shock, therefore, when I realized that my father's view of me was alloyed with reservations. I was, you might say, growing up. Things were made still more confusing by the attitude of my mother, who persisted in treating me with her old, unconditional approval, which she expressed with increasing warmth as my father's teasing became routine. A game was now under way. To show her that her approval was unjustified and inspired by maternal bias, my father kept a sharp lookout for my failings and follies, which he freely ridiculed. My mother, in her turn, would see no blemish in my character or appearance; a wilful blindness, as he saw it, that made him angry and jealous in equal parts. This is the kind of game only families can play; it has no winners, for everyone is a loser in the end, and there is no referee to blow a final whistle.

To make matters worse, my taste in books and pictures began to diverge from his, and although I was still unquestioningly conservative in most of my views he found himself increasingly out of sympathy with my aesthetic opinions. From the start, this conflict ran very deep on both sides. I can vividly recall an argument we had about Dickens, of all authors. He maintained that Dickens's reputation was quite unmerited and only kept alive through a conspiracy of academics and schoolmasters and their gullible pupils. Dickens, as anybody with any common sense could see, was 'crap'. Real people, he argued, enjoyed the kind of books written by C. S. Forester and Ed McBain (which I liked) and Alistair Maclean (which I didn't). The proof to him of their literary worth was the fact that they were best-sellers. But Dickens, I countered, was the most commercially successful author of his day and died a very rich man. His popularity was as great as his critical standing. My father would have none of this. Nobody would read his books today if they didn't have to. I said no more, for in fact I myself was reading Dickens for pleasure, along with the other 'classics' we were beginning to discover at school.

At the time these arguments confused and upset me, and it was some years before I saw how ludicrous it was that we were arguing at all. Most parents would have been delighted to find their child's nose buried in Dickens, but my father, having paid large sums of money to have me taught English literature, was annoyed when I turned round and liked the stuff. He thought me pretentious and easily led. I think he saw in my partiality for what he saw as high-falutin books the first sign that my education might not be taking me directly into a professional job. At all events, my new taste in reading annoyed and dispirited him, and our rows on the subject induced the first of the impassable silences which were later to become the grimmest feature of our relationship.

The ambivalence of my father's feelings was borne in on me by a set of remarks he used to make at the end of each holiday. He would take the opportunity when we were on our own to tell me what good company I had been during the past few weeks. I would glow. 'Much better company', he would add, 'than last holiday.' My glow would be dowsed. I would be left wondering glumly what it had been about my self of four months ago, from whom I felt no different, that was so unacceptable to him, and what it was about my present self that would no doubt be found inferior by next holiday.

It was around this time, during my first holidays from Shrewsbury, that I began to long in earnest to become someone I was not, to remake myself after an image of my own choosing, to re-invent myself. My father's teasing exacerbated this longing, but by no means caused it. Ever since I had been sent to prep school, my life had been a chaos of splittings and fractures. I was one person at home and another at school. At home, I dreaded returning to school; at school, I hankered to be at home. Later, this reversed itself, but the pattern of dislocation remained the same: wherever I was, I found myself an alien, and in the end I even felt an alien within my own body. My desire for a fresh persona was the product of all these fissures: I wanted a whole identity that would transcend them and leave me feeling at home with myself, if nowhere else. The problem was that apart from envying Kirk Douglas his chin, I had no idea who this new self was to be.

TEN

On the last night of the Easter term of 1960 I was corrupted, if not seduced, by two older boys.

These last nights of each term were made the occasion for innocuous saturnalia, which mostly consisted of staying up late to talk and to feast on biscuits by torchlight. Small quantities of alcohol were sometimes smuggled upstairs. I once bought a half-bottle of whisky and solemnly lay in my bed sipping it neat, gritting my teeth after every slug, until oblivion finally closed in.

On the night in question we were celebrating a term I had particularly enjoyed, not least because of the company pro-

vided by the others boys in my 'dorm'. Situated at the far end
of the house, with space for only six beds, it was more like a
bedroom than a school dormitory, and it offered a kind of
convivial intimacy impossible in the bigger rooms. I have quite
forgotten the monitor and the scum who slept there, but the
other three members of our party I remember well. Closest to
me in age, though slightly younger, was a likeable, straightforward boy, but I treated him condescendingly for I did not
want the other two older boys to identify me with him. I was
eager to be accepted by Moxon and Yates, who were in the
Lower Sixth, but such social climbing was not easily achieved
in a school where the barriers between generations were
rigidly upheld. In this case, my seniors proved to be a friendly
pair, not pompous about their rank, and I worked hard at
ingratiating myself. By the end of the term I was confident that
we had established an affable and democratic camaraderie.
My jokes and stories seemed to amuse them, and they in turn
talked freely in front of me.

Our last evening together as a group was balmy and
moonlit. The bedroom monitor, who was something of a bore,
soon fell asleep, as did the scum, despite his determination to
join in the revelry. Hinton, my contemporary, lay wakeful but
silent. Moxon had secreted a bottle of cider under his mattress,
and he shared it with Yates and myself. I was surprised and
flattered when my bed was chosen as the venue for our little
party. I was still more surprised and very shocked when I felt a
hand, Yates's hand, insinuate itself into my bed and slide
downwards. Not wishing to spoil our jolly mood, I shifted to
the other side of the bed, only to come abruptly into contact
with another hand, which was Moxon's.

Although I had some inkling of their motives, I really did not
know what in practice they were doing. I protested virginally
and dragged their arms out of my bed. They laughed with a
collusive glee that disturbed me, and returned to their siege on
my innocence.

'Relax,' said Yates silkily. 'You'll enjoy it. Leave it to us.'

'Haven't you done it before?' asked Moxon.

'No,' I shrilled with perfect honesty.

'It's much nicer when someone does it for you,' he said, not believing me. 'There. That's nice, isn't it?'

It was. But it was also shaming and very perplexing. I was overwhelmed by the classic conflicts of the seduced: I was offended by my friends' assault, mild and light-hearted though it was; I was hurt that they should treat me this way, exploiting and defiling our friendship; I wanted to resist, but was embarrassed to make a scene, especially since I suspected Hinton was listening; I did not want to offend my powerful, fascinating companions and I certainly did not want to make enemies of them with my obduracy; I was flattered by their interest in me, not so much out of sexual vanity, but because I calculated that their lust, if that was the word, would enhance the emotional ties between us; and finally, I was intrigued and excited and shiveringly pleased by the sensations they created whenever their practised fingers glided fleetingly across my burning penis. However, guilt proved to be the most powerful of all the emotions confusing me. I had some vague notion that sex was wrong under any circumstances, but I knew clearly that it was absolutely wrong between boys.

I continued to resist, therefore, and after a while, without taking offence, my would-be debauchers withdrew to their own beds. For all I know, they consoled each other. I, meanwhile, fell asleep, greatly relieved that I had escaped with both my virtue and my friendships intact. The next morning Moxon and Yates were as affable as ever and did not allude to the incident with so much as a glance or a smile. Only Hinton showed signs of being affected: from the whispered blandishments overheard in the dark he had obviously assumed that I had succumbed, and he glowered at me reproachfully, refusing to say goodbye as we all quit the bedroom for the last time. His look of disappointment made me feel momentarily ashamed, as if I had fallen and was tainted. But I soon recovered, for was I not innocent after all?

Technically, yes; but in a more significant sense my innocence had been depraved. A few nights later, lying in bed at home, I allowed my own hand to complete the work begun so enticingly by Moxon and Yates. Although I had been overtaken many times before by blameless orgasms in my sleep, I had not realized that the actual spasm itself was not merely a nice feeling, as promised by Moxon and inferred from the misty afterglow of wet dreams, but was an explosion of pure pleasure, the intensity of which was unmatched by any other sensual experience. I was instantly addicted, though that night I swore I would never do it again.

Not only had I inaugurated my sex life; I had also added another chamber to the house of secrets, the invisible annexe to my parents' home, to which I withdrew more and more as my adolescence proceeded.

That last night of the summer term had other repercussions. The following term I found myself in a much larger bedroom which contained no particular friends of mine, of any age. One night during the second or third week I woke to find Yates sitting on the chair beside my bed, his hand already beneath the sheets. Before I could move his fingers possessed me, and I simply capitulated, unable either to enjoy or to resist. When it was over, he disappeared without a word. He returned half a dozen times that term; I never refused him, he never asked me to reciprocate, and we never exchanged a word. I could not understand what satisfaction he derived from these sorties, which for him resulted in nothing more gratifying than a strictly vicarious relief, and I never asked him. Our friendship of the previous term withered and we could hardly look each other in the eye during the day. After a while his midnight visits ceased, without comment or explanation, and I was only thankful.

The mind has an extraordinary capacity to lock up and

ignore ideas that are potentially disturbing. In so far as I thought about my liaison with Yates at all, I thought of it as something quite unconnected with homosexuality. There were boys who affected, and some who sincerely felt, great passions for younger boys – 'tea-boys' – and sighed for them, wrote them billets-doux, made assignations and generally carried on like Elizabethan lovers. There were others who claimed to be overpowered with lust for pretty boys and longed to 'rape' them. I was never to experience any such feelings, all of which struck me as bad translations of those I was beginning to feel very intensely for girls. Nor did Yates appear to hold me in any kind of romantic esteem. As far as I was concerned, he was no more than a third hand. I felt neither affection nor desire for him. He fulfilled his strange function more or less mechanically, and while he was at work guilt and gratification mixed themselves in proportions that made it just possible to let him continue. Despite the fact that my sexual initiation was at his hands, so to speak, my fantasies remained resolutely concerned with women, and it was at about this time that I discovered the far more rewarding, indeed compulsive, stimulus to be found in magazines.

Towards Moxon, who was by now a monitor, my feelings were different, for in him I discerned a kindness Yates had never shown. One evening towards the end of that autumn term, I saw him go upstairs and followed him. It was a rule, only loosely enforced, that the upper floor of the house was out of bounds during the day, so there was a chance of a moment's privacy. I found him in his dormitory and, as much to my own surprise as to his, I made a blind, sobbing lurch towards him, trying to embrace him, or rather trying to get him to embrace me. He repulsed me violently and ran from the room, red with anger and embarrassment. He never spoke to me again; nor, to give him his due, did he ever punish me for my folly.

I had been driven to this clumsy, futile gesture not out of any sexual impulse, but out of a pathetic desire to have an older person, a parental substitute, show me some affection. I simply wanted to be hugged. I do not know how Moxon, poor fellow, interpreted my sudden show of emotion, but he wanted none of it. I have forgotten what private crisis prompted me to take this desperate step, though I do recall being shocked by the violence of my feelings and the suddenness with which they had welled up. They were of course as quickly subdued and sealed over.

It was always a source of satisfaction, even of complacency, to my parents that when I was asked what I wanted to be after I left school, I always answered without hesitation that I was going to be a solicitor. They would point, a little scornfully, at other boys who mumbled and dithered in response to this question, and congratulate themselves on my good sense.

By the time the question was beginning to acquire more than just conversational interest, my father's own career was thriving and there was every likelihood that he would in due course become the senior partner of his firm – as indeed he did. My grandfather had not yet retired from the bench and behind him lay the precedents of his father and his father-in-law, both of whom had been eminent and wealthy solicitors in Liverpool. I had been born into a legal dynasty, and it was my family's reasonable hope that I would take my place in this glorious succession.

My firm reply as to my chosen destiny also reassured my parents that the large sums of money they were spending on my education were being well invested. Had I replied that my ambition was to be a doctor, dentist or any kind of professional with a qualification 'behind him', they would have been almost as content. Indeed, they told me that I should be in no haste to commit myself. Even if I did choose the law, a wealth of choice was still before me: I could become either a barrister or a solicitor. Were I to opt for the latter, a place might be made for me in my father's firm, but either way I could expect to inherit all the advantages of possessing a long-established and honourable legal name.

In point of fact, I never gave much thought to this great issue. My future seemed to be more my parents' business than mine, and I gave my careless consent to their vision of it. I passed my exams with relative ease, I did more or less as I was told by my parents and teachers alike, and my life seemed to be coasting smoothly towards the golden prospect everyone had mapped out for me. I occasionally visited my father's office, which looked an agreeable place, and as a special treat I was taken once or twice by my mother to observe the spectacle of His Honour, my grandfather, presiding over his court, awesomely dressed in wig and scarlet robes. The court usher would fussily escort us to our seats on the visitors' bench, the wig would bow graciously in our direction, and we would enjoy a comfortable shiver of fear, knowing that power was smiling covertly on us. From the little I saw of it, the law looked congenial enough, and anyway it cost me nothing to please my parents by saying I wanted to follow in the family tradition.

But then, during the summer of my sixteenth year, my untroubled, unthinking ascension towards the throne of the law was suddenly interrupted. I read a certain book. There was nothing in its title to suggest a revolutionary work, but it changed my life as surely as the Bible and *Das Kapital* have changed those of other people. I still have the copy I read then, a Pelican edition priced 3/6, and I can remember when and even where I read it. Most keenly of all, I remember *how* I read it – with uncontainable excitement.

The book was *The Aesthetic Adventure* by William Gaunt. Published originally in 1945, it is the most readable and evocative account I know of the so-called Aesthetic movement in England during the later nineteenth century. It is not so much a cultural history as a multiple biography of the many colourful and doomed figures who wrote and painted during that period, notably Rossetti, Ruskin, Swinburne, Pater, Whistler and Wilde. In a way, it is a portrait of London too, or rather of the bohemian London of the time; and there among the raffish squalor and soiled elegance which Gaunt had conjured up so vividly, I found my spiritual home.

Like generations of public-school boys before me, consigned to all-male institutions where the Victorian ethos still hung in a slowly shredding fog around neo-Gothic buildings, I identified far too ardently with the Decadents and their shameless city. I longed to return to the London where Ernest Dowson might be found languishing in Soho, crying for madder music and stronger wine; to the Mile End Road (wherever that was) to buy a match from the disgraced and drunken Simeon Solomon; to Vigo Street, glowing wickedly with copies of the *Yellow Book*; to Sickert's Camden Town with its music halls, murderers and *demi-monde*.

The London of my dreams was peopled entirely with Gaunt's extraordinary poets and painters, the like of whom I had never read about before. Dandified or ragged, celebrated or obscure, broken by impossible loves for unattainable mistresses or debauched by all too attainable boyfriends, Gaunt's aesthetic adventurers were united, it seemed, by being romantically damned, one and all, to early deaths. If poor health did not kill them, they killed themselves, or simply expired through a sheer inability to meet the demands of ordinary middle-class existence.

Indoors, mine was a black-and-white London, erotically decorated by Beardsley, the boy consumptive; outdoors, it was a London shrouded in the grey mist of a Whistler nocturne. There were no daylight hours here, for it was Thomson's 'City of Dreadful Night', where the baroque crimes of Dorian Gray and Mr Hyde might well have baffled even Sherlock Holmes's giant brain. It was a London of streets and public places, rather than houses and homes, its cafés patronized by wits, its

pavements haunted by prostitutes and rent-boys, its very gut-
ters choked with drunken genius. Above all, it was the London
of Oscar Wilde – of Tite Street ringing with ridiculous epigrams,
of the Café Royal's mirrored and marbled hospitality, of St
James's Theatre and triumphant first nights, of the Savoy Hotel
and feasts with panthers, and finally of the Old Bailey.

How could any neurotic adolescent worthy of the name fail
to be excited by all this histrionic self-destruction, all these
sublime falls from grace? In my case, I was not merely excited, I
was metamorphosed. I put down the book knowing exactly
what I wanted to be (not, mark you, what I wanted to *do*): I
wanted to be a writer; or, more frankly, a genius.

Whether out of *naïveté* or ignorance, I had not realized before
reading Gaunt's book that it was possible to exist as an artist
alone, to be identifiable in adulthood as someone who wrote,
painted, or whatever, and did nothing else. Not that I was much
interested in the economics of it, but I had not realized that
people could and did live by their creative wits, unsupported by
'proper' jobs or private money. Once I had grasped it, however,
the idea seemed to me the most exhilarating and profound I had
ever come across, and it still does. I was convinced that to devote
oneself to a life of the imagination was the highest possible
aspiration, beside which everything else paled into triviality.
For me, the only conceivable means of imaginative expression
was writing, and I knew now that if I were to do anything other
than write, I would be no more than half-alive. Where the
strength of this conviction came from, I do not know, for I had
not previously held firm opinions or entertained immovable
beliefs. But the fact is that from the moment I closed Gaunt's not
notably inspirational book I was filled with an absolute certainty of my mission, which I could not wait to fulfil. That sense
of certainty and of haste has never since deserted me.

At that time my fantasies were embodied in the figure of
Oscar Wilde; he became my hero and his was the style of life I
most wanted to emulate. I was not attracted to his homosexu-

ality, which was interesting only in so far as it gave his story the shape of a Greek tragedy. What fascinated me was his superb confidence, his flamboyant air of being a self-crowned king, his genial assumption of superiority, by virtue of nothing but his wit and genius, over the ordinary, fuddy-duddy world. I saw myself as a dandy and *flâneur* like him; I too would stroll down Piccadilly, or some such fashionable street (my knowledge of London was very hazy), tossing quips at booksellers as they filled their windows with my novels and books of poetry, and bowing to theatre managers as they pasted 'house full' notices on the bills of my brilliant comedies. I too would be lionized by beautiful women, and hear my *bons mots* repeated round the salons of Mayfair. I would outrage the pompous, shock the prudish and, to use a quintessential phrase of the period, *épater le bourgeois*. And I would be the broken and tragic victim of my own (unspecified) follies. In short, I longed to out-Oscar Oscar.

I could hardly have been introduced to *la vie de bohème* by a more destructive book than Gaunt's – destructive, that is, to my intended career as a lawyer. In their frequent clashes with society, it was the law, as often as not, which brought about the downfalls of my new heroes. Both Whistler and Wilde fell foul of the law when they brought their ill-judged libel suits, and both were cruelly punished for their impertinence. To me, the law was not an ass; I knew too much about it to think that. Certainly in Gaunt's melodramas, it was the official voice of respectability sounding its fruitiest tone, as well as the flat-footed agent of philistinism, but it was also powerful and dangerous. If anything, Gaunt glamorized the law by turning the dreary business of cross-examination into a swashbuckling duel between the aesthetic rapier and the legal sabre. Yet who, given the choice at fifteen, would seek to follow the joyless Carson, Wilde's lethal adversary, in favour of Oscar himself? Not I, at any rate.

Without thinking it through in any organized, defiant way, I came to realize that the world of my father and grandfather, to which I had been committing myself so casually all these years, was in fact one I did not want to join. I did not confide this in anyone, for there was nothing to confide: the future was a very distant prospect, still not to be taken seriously. After all, writing could not be reduced to something as tiresome as a career, requiring exams and qualifications and references. It was a glorious destiny, which in my own good time I would gloriously fulfil. Meanwhile, I became more and more heavily addicted to my new drug, and nobody, least of all I myself, considered the consequences.

Nor did I make any effort for another year to test my vainglorious fantasies against the reality of talent. My Pelican copy of Hesketh Pearson's effervescent biography of Wilde has the date August 1960 written on the flyleaf, together with two slightly different signatures and my two addresses, home and school. This announcement of dual nationality, so to speak, reads to me now as if it were an unconscious attempt to yoke together my two contrary spheres of existence, but maybe I am psychologising after the event. In any case, it was not until July 1961 that my first published work, a poem of some forty-one lines, appeared in the school magazine. This set an intoxicating precedent, because the poem was also the first piece I had deliberately written in the hope of publication. I felt a great pride and astonishment when the editor, who never spoke to me again, and had assuredly never spoken to me before, told me casually one morning outside the chapel that he had space for my contribution.

'Good effort,' he drawled, and strolled away.

My poem contained the following immortal lines:

'The orchid has a strange, perfumed, evil beauty;
But the smell and feel of honest sweat is beautiful, is fine.'

I had never smelt an orchid, evil or otherwise, and my experience of sweating, when pounding round on one of our dreaded compulsory runs for example, was that it was quite the opposite of beautiful and fine. But I was concerned with literature, not life, and if sentiments of this kind were good enough for Wilde and Hemingway, they were good enough for me.

I was steeped in Hemingway at the time, for his work was used by our English master to illustrate the latter's extraordinary theory that stories by good writers were written with the intention of expressing . . . a theme. Incredulous, we gasped at the absurdity of it. Stories were stories, weren't they? Events happened, people spoke to each other, places got described and then, if the story was any good, all these things came to an exciting ending. *Themes* – we spoke the word in our most sarcastic tone – were invented by *critics* – contemptible parasites – who forced them on to stories, but they had nothing to do with what the writer was thinking when he sat down to tell his tale. And so the argument raged. The master stuck to his preposterous theory, making us read story after story to prove it, and we resisted it just as obstinately.

One day, I suddenly understood that he was right. Stories were not just action and character and background; they were ideas too. It was not perhaps easy to see this in Hemingway, because the action and atmosphere were usually so compelling, but what was *Dorian Grey* if not a novel of ideas? I immediately became one of the master's few allies in the class.

On the strength of our new solidarity, I saw him at the end of a lesson and asked him if he would use one of Wilde's stories as an example.

'Oscar Wilde', he said to me witheringly, 'is something you grow out of.'

I was stunned; not so much by his judgement on Wilde – I was far too fanatical a disciple to take that seriously – as by his dereliction of duty. Here was I, a reformed barbarian, positively asking to share in the culture he had hitherto been preaching to deaf ears, and all he could do was patronize me. I guessed he had a suspicion that my interest in Wilde was more homosexual than literary, but even so his response was hardly fair. My obsession with Wilde, now goaded by a pleasant sense of persecution, became even more consuming.

As a footnote, I can report that this teacher subsequently deserted both England and her literature for the mystic East. Swathed in orange robes, he now sits at the feet of a guru in an ashram somewhere in India, undisturbed by the pesterings of decadent schoolboys.

During the holiday of that same summer, I experienced the pangs of love for the first time, and very painful they were too.

By then my Stackpole grandmother had been dead for nearly two years, and my grandfather had decided to employ a housekeeper. For some reason his choice landed on a Belgian girl, one Erica, the daughter of a Brussels industrialist, whom my parents and I first met when we went to Stackpole in August for our usual biannual holiday. Despite the moment-ous part she was to play in my sentimental education, I have only the haziest mental picture of her: aged about twenty-one, she was small, dark and somewhat weasel-faced, with a determined, intense manner. She also suffered from a slight stoop.

She was no beauty, but she possessed a forceful personality, and for a while she successfully held the entire family in her thrall. Perhaps we all deferred subconsciously to the streak of sadism in her character; certainly my grandfather, that lion of authority, appeared to be cowed by her, and the rest of us took our tune from him.

I have since been told that by the time we arrived she was already causing trouble on the farm, but if my parents discussed her behaviour with my uncle and aunt they did so out of my hearing. None of us could avoid noticing one aspect of her perversity, however, and that was her treatment of my grandfather's dog, which was a corgi. The creature was unusually nervous, even by the standards of its breed, and it amused Erica to trap it in the dining-room when my grandfather was out of the way and torment it by tapping the lid of a silver teapot, for which noise it had conceived a terrible dread. The wretched dog would shiver and whine, rushing to the door and yelping to be released. Erica would laugh quite shamelessly, expecting us to find its sufferings as comical as she did. The corgi was also terrified of water, so whenever we were at the beach Erica did not hesitate to carry it out to sea, holding it just above the waves where it wriggled and cried in a frenzy of fear. Although we were all rather appalled by her cruelty, I do not remember that anyone tried to stop her.

In her day, my grandmother had run the house along old-fashioned lines, demanding a certain degree of respectful formality from everyone in her employ, and it therefore came as a shock to find that in the kitchen Erica had installed a gramophone and a large collection of pop records which she played loudly and repetitively. The cook used to get furious with what she saw as Erica's impudence, but the rest of us, who did not have to work with her, came to welcome this new gaiety in a room that had always been somewhat sombre. Her taste in music was unexpectedly sentimental, her favourite being the ineffable 'Why Must I Be A Teenager In Love?' As she listened to these tragic ditties, she would dance, holding herself round her bony shoulders and singing in a coyly suggestive tone. It was hot that summer and the big window where she kept her gramophone was always open, allowing the sound of her records and the sight of her wistful performances to be noticed from the farmyard and its buildings.

I do not know if these tricks were intended for anyone in particular, but they exercised a magical fascination over me. I became acutely conscious of Erica's presence, watching her all the time and catching her eye whenever I could. She responded by exchanging special glances with me. I contrived to be with her at every opportunity and she seemed to relish our little moments together. One afternoon, when the rest of the household were elsewhere, she invited me to dance with her. She put on a record, placed my arms round her, laughed at my clumsiness, and then drew me closer. And so my first dance culminated in my first kiss.

The record finished and teasingly she broke away to change it. Before we could resume our dancing, one of the maids came into the room. Without a glance in my direction, Erica immediately began to talk to her, behaving as if nothing had happened and leaving me stunned and frantic.

From that moment onwards I was of course helplessly infatuated. I followed Erica everywhere, thinking of nothing except ways to be alone with her and kiss her again. She allowed me to snatch occasional and maddeningly brief embraces. Mostly, however, she toyed with my ardour. For whole days she would refuse to answer my pining looks and would evade my clumsy caresses, and then, just as my despondency was reaching suicidal intensity, she would pinch me secretly, or blow in my ear when nobody was looking, or let her hand fall on mine for a moment, squeezing it collusively and reviving all my rapturous hopes. Though I suspected she was making a fool of me, I was too inexperienced to know it for sure and too drunk with sexual expectation to care.

After a while I must have become more insistent, because she agreed to meet me early one morning, before anyone else was awake, in the grain store which overlooked the little yard outside the dairy and was well away from the house. The choice of rendezvous was hers, and the privacy it guaranteed naturally gave me the impression that at last our relationship was going to develop beyond kissing. I hardly slept the night before and was dressed an hour before dawn. I did not hear her leave her room, but sure enough she was in the kitchen waiting for me when I came down. Hand in hand we slipped out of the house, across the main yard and up the wooden steps that led into the barn. In the dusty half-dark we lay down on a bed of sacks and began to kiss with the furious passion that had become our habit.

The gymnastics of lovemaking were as yet still a mystery to me, in terms both of technique and of etiquette, but as soon as one of my hands became free, I burrowed urgently, while still kissing Erica, down the front of her blouse in the direction of her breast. I was astounded to feel my wrist grabbed and halted. Applying irresistible strength, she clamped me in a wrestler's hold that left my face accessible and utterly immobilized the rest of me. Thus paralyzed, I was forced to continue with our kissing until it was time to leave the barn.

We retired to the barn on several subsequent mornings but, sad to say, my initiation was to proceed no further than this high-pressure kissing, which by being so fervent and yet so unprogressive amounted almost to a perversion in Erica. To this day, I have no idea what satisfaction she derived from our face-to-face writhings, or, for that matter, what her feelings were for me.

We found one other opportunity to be alone together and that was during a beach party arranged for the teenagers of the village. The night was mild and Erica and I lay in each other's arms, after our erogenously chaste fashion, on the crest of a sand-dune looking down on the beach where a bonfire had been lit and the village kids were necking and drinking beer. In an attempt to impress her, I talked about my ambitions to be a lawyer. As it happened, this was the first proper conversation we had had, but although I struggled to wax eloquent on the subject of my glowing legal future, my heart was not in it; indeed, this must have been the last occasion on which I linked my destiny to the law with any attempt at sincerity. I was in any case scoring no points with Erica, who had suffered her fill of lawyers and other such bourgeois hopefuls in Brussels. I had not shown her my volume of Wilde's *Collected Works* which, together with her body, was my obsession for that August, and

I did not mention my new-found literary heroes during this autobiographical chat on the beach. This may well have been a mistake, because all those suicides, neurotics and drunkards would probably have appealed to her much more than lawyers, and my identification with them might have told in my favour.

Despite my best endeavours, I was still a virgin at the end of our fortnight's stay at Stackpole. Nevertheless, I was in love; and not merely in love, but desperate to be married to my inamorata. There was, to my mind, no break in the emotional chain which connected sexual desire with infatuation with love with marriage – and there never has been. As the last day of our holiday came closer my fantasy of married life with Erica, whom I kept quite ignorant of my schemes, grew more elaborate and felt ever more concrete. I imagined conversations with her hard-headed industrialist father in which I brilliantly annihilated his objections to the age difference between us and the trifling matter of my lack of income.

Then one morning we drove out of the farmyard, our holiday at an end. Erica did not come to the door to wave us off; nor, as I had hoped she would, had she found the opportunity to give me a farewell kiss. On the contrary, she had avoided me, leaving me to listen mournfully to 'Why Must I Be A Teenager In Love?' for the last time. Nothing had been said between us; not a word for me to take away and console myself with during the coming ordeal of our separation, not a word to confirm that ours was in truth a Great Romance. I tried to conceal my tears from my parents as we drove towards Pembroke. I had not felt such pain since I had first been parted from my parents at prep school.

Back at home, I wrote Erica a letter; an impassioned, extravagant letter in which I described my plans for our future together and begged her for a photograph of herself or some little token (like my rubber mouse) that I might keep as a tangible reminder of her. Day after day I waited for her reply. It never came.

ELEVEN

The breaking of my heart became an annual ritual. My parents could now afford foreign holidays and the following summer we flew to Ventimiglia, an Italian seaside resort close to the French border. On the beach in front of our hotel I met Natalia, known as 'Tati' to her innumerable younger sisters. Within an hour or so, and despite our lack of a mutual language, I was profoundly in love with her. Throughout the ensuing fortnight we were chaperoned everywhere by her chubby sister Olga, who was fortunately much more interested in ice-cream than in policing our behaviour. Tati gave me to understand that my feelings for her were to some degree reciprocated. Once more I was afflicted with marital fantasies; once more I suffered an agonizing separation; once more my love letter went unanswered.

Another year went by before I found myself once again in a social situation where girls were painlessly accessible. I did not waste my opportunity. That summer my paternal grandfather took us on a cruise, installing my parents somewhat anachronistically in the bridal cabin. At sea I lost my heart to a Dutch girl, Marije. Having been emotionally half-starved for so long, I gorged myself. I had no powers of self-restraint nor of self-protection; I knew no caution and hoped for nothing less than a commitment for life from my beloved. She did not give it, but she did at least write to me occasionally from her home in Hilversum.

Though my holiday romances were exceedingly ardent, they were, notwithstanding every blandishment I could devise, blamelessly chaste. I was, however, no longer a virgin. Some nine months after my 'affair' with Erica my sentimental education had moved on to a higher grade when I was taken to a prostitute in London by a friend, who had himself discovered the existence of such women only that week.

Under his escort, I went to Old Compton Street and walked through a doorway which had a card advertising 'Simone' pinned to its battered portico. Painted on the pediment above was a pair of rosy, dimpling goddesses, suitably naked, who held up a garland of letters spelling out the words 'Venus Social Rooms'. I was reassured and excited by the suggestion of Victorian decadence they exuded, though I later discovered the 'Rooms' were no more than a clip joint. At the top of the stairs I found a doorbell in Simone's name, but was trembling so violently I had to press it with my elbow.

After some time the door was opened and I found myself in a little room made hot and damp by the steam gushing from a kettle.

'Allo darleeng! I be with you in two minutes.'

A woman, presumably Simone, disappeared into the room next door, and I was left to meditate on a glimpse of black nylon and white skin spiced with a pungent whiff of some musky perfume. I was also left to enjoy the company of the 'maid'. My friend had told me that a maid would probably be in attendance, and I had assumed this person would be a sort of apprentice tart, a saucy figure in a naughty uniform hovering in the background and adding somehow to the revels. I was therefore very surprised to be offered a cup of tea by an old-age pensioner wearing fingerless gloves, fluffy slippers and an entire jumble sale of cardigans buttoned one on top of another. In spite of the oppressive heat thrown out by the gas fire, her knuckles and the tip of her nose were cruelly empurpled, and she hugged her bones in a vain attempt to warm them. She poured the tea, ladling quantities of sugar into both our mugs, and muttered wheezingly about the state of the weather and the world, both of which were in her view highly. unsatisfactory. A canary fluttered round the room, settling occasionally on her head. There was nothing in her manner, in her conversation, in her behaviour or in the décor of the room to indicate the reality of our situation; I might have been a nephew paying a duty visit to a mildly senile aunt. I struggled to be polite to her, while trying all the time to catch a sound from next door, but I only heard a few shrill sounds from Simone which I could not interpret.

At last I heard the rattling of a door opening and closing, and footsteps banging down the stairs. My turn had come. Shaking with fear, I waited for Simone to call me in; I suffered a sensation uncomfortably reminiscent of waiting outside the headmaster's study at prep school. At this moment the canary hopped on to my shoulder, lifted its tail and dropped a juicy deposit on my tweed jacket. The bedroom door opened and Simone beckoned me within.

My visit was not a success, but the next day I returned and made another attempt. The earth did not move – indeed I did not feel much pleasure at all – but now I could at least claim in all honesty that I had done it.

I had been worried about the canary dropping on my jacket and how to explain it away, but within an hour or so it had dried out and was easily brushed off, leaving not a trace. And so, at first, it seemed to be with the experience itself. No guilty stain was left to tell the wicked story; no mark of sin was branded on my forehead; nothing remained to betray where I had been or what I had done. In fact the experience was not so easily erased; on the contrary, I lived with its consequences for many years.

I had expected my friend to brag about our escapade, as I planned to do, when we returned to school, but in the event neither of us mentioned it, even between ourselves. Looking back, as I constantly did, I found that my feelings were very confused. I was proud of having dared to do something unusual and outrageous, especially since it had a touch of 'nineties *nostalgie de la boue* about it, fuelling my already heated identification with Degas, Toulouse-Lautrec and the other men of their period who seemed to have been more at home in the brothel than the drawing-room. Nor was I troubled with any sense of having done wrong, far less of having committed a sin. This was not surprising. The only sexual morality we had ever been taught was confined to the Seventh Commandment, which was hardly applicable to us, since adultery was a far more ambitious project than any of us had in mind. We just wanted to get into bed with a girl. It was tacitly assumed that we understood fornication to be wrong, and definitely against school rules, and there the matter was left.

Though I felt some pride and next to no guilt, I was conscious of having isolated myself still further from the world of ordinary girls by my foray on Soho. I had had sex, but that was all, for it had not brought me any closer to getting to know a girl. I had undergone an experience beyond my years, inappropriate to my age. I had discovered that sex was something you could simply go out and purchase, bypassing all the agonies, frustrations and defeats of teenage seduction, about which I knew very little and longed to know more. By taking a short cut round these difficulties and buying my conquest, I had not only cheated, something I felt keenly, but – much worse – I had also separated off sex from the rest of my life, making it a thing in itself, disconnected from my everyday social relationships and doomed to exist only in secrecy. Furthermore, the actual sex I had known was now dissociated even from my sexual fantasies. True, these were somewhat overshadowed by Simone's unforgettable features, especially her rich black hairiness and tangy, damp skin, for which no soft-porn photograph could have prepared me, but I still dreamed of making love to and just going out with a girl of my own age.

Alas, apart from my annual exposure to foreign elements, I very seldom met any girls, and I had left school before I first took a girl out in Liverpool. Invitations did occasionally come my way, and I remember one party, a barn dance, with especial sharpness because it took place when my bite from the fruit of sexual knowledge was still fresh in my mouth. It proved to be a dance in a real barn, and as the evening wore on a mild orgy developed among the straw bales. I did not dance once; I did not talk to anyone and nobody talked to me. Instead, I glowered in a corner, the smouldering coal of my lust fanned by self-pity. No doubt I managed to look forbidding and superior, but a few astute souls must have seen me for what I was: wretched, gauche, and too neurotic to be anything but dull company.

Back at school, even the most innocent contact with a girl was impossible to contrive, and was in any case virtually a capital offence. This enforced exile from ordinary social experience fostered the growth of the most ludicrous misapprehensions. Among these was the idea that girls were essentially primitive creatures, savages decked out in paint, flowers and trinkets, who were to be tricked or bribed into surrendering their bodies. The impression that they were passive objects of desire, who were almost insensible to the lust they aroused, was all too easily formed in the mind of someone whose relations with them were largely confined to looking at the pictures in pornographic magazines. Such was the perverse effect of my single-sex upbringing that I came to see flesh-and-blood girls as shadows of the ever-willing images smiling from the pages of *Parade* and *Playboy*. Becoming the client of a prostitute was only a short step from buying these pictures, but making any kind of fulfilled relationship with a real girl seemed a very distant prospect.

One day, when I was fifteen or sixteen, my father opened the door of my room to find me staring soulfully into the mirror and reciting Hamlet's famous soliloquy after the manner of Olivier at his most yearning. I do not know whether he heard the words or, if he heard them, whether he recognized the speech and guessed I was imitating Olivier whose records I played with obsessive frequency, but he heard and saw enough to get the point. Here was yet another illustration of the lamentable course my intellectual development was taking (though 'intellectual' was not a word he would have used). I had filled my head with 'a boatload of nonsense', or, to give things their proper name, 'crap' (the word he always used to denounce high culture).

He stood in the doorway and we confronted each other's reflections for a moment; mine a crumbling mask of embarrassment, his a study in amused contempt. He closed the door with an air of exaggerated discretion.

But he did not know the half of it. How could he? How

could my mother either, for that matter? For I never disclosed the content of my internal life to them, far less discussed it, and without some knowledge of the fantasies that ruled my thinking they could not possibly have been expected to understand me.

My second-hand rendition of Hamlet's speech owed less to an identification with the Brooding Dane than to one with Olivier himself. I hero-worshipped Olivier on account of his portrayal of Richard III, with whom in turn I identified most powerfully. My father might just as easily have caught me in the midst of that other soliloquy, 'Now is the winter of our discontent . . .' which Olivier had made almost equally famous. I had learnt the words off the record and knew them by heart, as well as every pause, inflection and climax. Time and again I dragged my club foot round the room, my shoulder twisted into a hump, my left arm dangling uselessly, my head screwed up at a malevolent angle, and repeated those gloriously evil lines in the curious steely, strangulated voice Olivier had concocted for what was surely his best performance.

At that time, and for some years to come, I lived almost entirely on a plane of imaginative self-projection: I hardly existed at all in my own right, but was forever metamorphosing myself into one or other of the many heroes I worshipped. Like a religious fanatic, I not only strove in each case to follow in the footsteps of my master, but longed to shed my own unworthy self and actually become the godhead. While awaiting the final transubstantiation, I made myself an expert in their holy texts and turned my room into a shrine for their sacred relics. It was in the nature of my confusion concerning my own identity that I could not even fix on one god in whose image I would remake myself; I had a dozen, and even had it been possible for the butterflies of fantasy to emerge from the grubs of adolescent desire, my scheme for self-transformation was doomed to abort through sheer inconsistency.

Most of my heroes were writers and painters, and further-more all suffered some form of disablement, either physical or psychological. For instance, like all my generation, I was a great admirer of the Impressionists, and I felt definite pangs of identification with Gauguin and Van Gogh rather than with the more balanced and professionally successful Monet and Renoir. But my most ardent devotion was reserved for the stunted denizen of brothels, Toulouse-Lautrec, who was in his way the ultimate outsider, the hero as cripple. Among the poets, I of course read the Romantics. My favourite as a poet was Coleridge, but it was the club-footed, infamous Byron who most fascinated me. I amassed a large library of biographical material about him; but it was typical of my mania that I should have been wholly preoccupied with the man at the expense of the artist, for although I became quite knowledgeable about Byron's life story, I never actually read his work.

When I discovered the 1890s, which amounted to an entire generation of cripples, I flung myself into so promiscuous an orgy of identification it is a wonder I survived with my sanity intact. As I have already described, Oscar Wilde was the figure with whom I felt the keenest affinity, seeing him as tragically and splendidly crippled by his homosexuality. My predilection for monstrosities led me unerringly to Quasimodo, to Shake-speare's Crouchback, to Cyrano de Bergerac, but for some reason not to Quilp of *The Old Curiosity Shop*. I did, however, respond to Sydney Carton, the dissolute and alcoholic anti-hero of *A Tale of Two Cities*. He was irresistibly interesting on two extra counts, as 'old Sydney Carton of old Shrewsbury School' and as a barrister. By this time I was beginning to find my legal career an almost inconceivable prospect, but Carton, making his way home at dawn stealthily and unsteadily, like a dissolute cat, was the kind of barrister I could emulate. He was a hero by virtue of having unheroic qualities, and it was not his moment of masochistic glory on the scaffold steps as he prepared to do his far, far better thing that appealed to me; it was his self-destructive nights in the Temple and his insatiable thirst for bumpers of punch. 'The sun', wrote Dickens, 'rose on no sadder sight than the man of good abilities and good emotions, incapable of their directed exercise, incapable of his own help and his own happiness, sensible of the blight on him, and resigning himself to let it eat him away.' This was my kind of hero – bathos and all.

My pantheon included one other major god: Marlon Brando, or rather the Brando of a particular film – *One-Eyed Jacks* which he starred in and directed. This was the only film I ever saw in a Shrewsbury cinema, for we were as strictly forbidden to enter cinemas as pubs, and the punishment for both these heinous crimes was the same: a severe caning, of which I was mightily frightened. The film, for those unfortunate enough to have missed it, was a western set in spectacular scenery around Monterey, California, and a classic story of vengeance and romance. It contained a scene of extremely realistic cruelty in which the Brando character was whipped by Karl Malden, the sheriff, who had once been Brando's buddy and partner in crime. To ensure that his old friend's gun-slinging days were finally over, and by way of a little self-protection, the sheriff completed the beating by smashing Brando's shooting hand with the stock of a rifle. The rest of the film concerned Brando's efforts to secure revenge. From the moment I tottered out of that cinema, and for the next two or three years, I wanted nothing so much as to be Brando. There is nothing unusual in a teenager looking up to and even wanting to imitate a film star, though the strength of my imitative passion may have been rather less common, but what *was* strange was my identification with the maimed, damaged Brando to the exclusion of all the other, far more glamorous roles he played. Or should I say personae he offered?

I was not content simply to dream myself into the beings of these super-heroes that were bursting through the bars of my overcrowded skull. Wherever possible, I tried to assume their mantles, or at least to wear a badge or some other insignia to bring myself within their aura. For instance, at the height of my Brando cult, I took to sporting a quite redundant thumb-sling in imitation of the one he had worn while recovering the use of his hand in *One-Eyed Jacks*. I also wrapped myself in a long, floating silk scarf like his, and I would sit, whenever I remembered to, in an attitude of exaggerated virility, my face cemented into a Brandoesque expression of brooding intensity, hoping that others would react to me as I had reacted to him. I did not, however, have the courage to adopt his curious nasal intonation, nor to address people as 'scum-sucking pigs' or make use of other such choice phrases drawn from the vocabulary of the film, though they reverberated constantly in my head.

In an effort to transmute myself into Toulouse-Lautrec I once groped my way round Liverpool half-blinded by a pair of pince-nez. (I could hardly have shuffled about on my knees, although I dare say I considered it.) On another occasion I shocked the lady at the box-office of Stratford's Royal Shakespeare Theatre by hauling myself across the foyer with a limp that appeared to be so agonizing she rushed to help me, solicitously holding my withered arm while I staggered and crumpled at every broken step. She only became suspicious when I asked for my tickets in a voice which unmistakably echoed Olivier's.

In the guise of Oscar Wilde I affected a cane and a cigarette-holder; as Sherlock Holmes (another hero disabled from within) I wore the obligatory deerstalker; and in an effort to imitate Dirk Bogarde's indolent Carton I trained myself to hang my eyelids at a drooping half-mast. Despite all this theatricality, I was not a flamboyant boy – indeed I was positively inhibited – and these gestures were therefore executed with a scurrying furtiveness. I certainly tried never to betray a hint to my parents of my excursions into these *alter egos*.

Only once did I indulge in an act of exhibitionism which was
so outrageous and manifestly neurotic that it frightened even
me. One winter's day I took the ferry across the river to
Birkenhead, which I did not know well and where I was quite
unknown. I was wearing a long black overcoat which I had
recently inherited from my Stackpole grandfather, who had
died in the December of 1963 – I was nineteen. I found my way
into a large covered market and wandered about for a while,
feeling sick and agitated. Finally I went into a café, where,
without any premeditation, I began to shamble and drool as if
I were half-witted. Dragging my feet and mumbling volubly, I
approached the counter and in a barely intelligible voice
demanded a cup of tea. The entire place fell silent as I fumbled
cretinously for money, which was refused by the waitress, and
slopped my tea in an effort to drink it with drivelling lips. To
everyone's relief, I tottered out at last and found a corner
where I could resume my ordinary self – if such an entity
existed by then.

Apart from inspiration very loosely derived from Dostoev-
sky's Prince Myshkin, the holy fool and epileptic hero of *The
Idiot*, I have no idea what prompted this impersonation of an
imbecile, which in retrospect brought me nothing but shame. I
was extremely anxious to be anyone except the person I was,
but I did not know who I wanted to become, or who it was, for
that matter, I was longing to discard. I thought I might induce
a sudden revolution through some physical means, through a
convulsive paroxysm akin to an epileptic fit, which like a
geological upheaval would convert the existing materials of
my self into a completely new form. The inside would be
turned out, the exterior would be rendered unrecognizable,
and irresistible energies would be unleashed. I could never at
the time have articulated my hopes so clearly or dispassion-
ately, but I certainly cherished a belief in the galvanizing
ipower of some such cataclysm.

As well as feeling ashamed and disturbed after the Birkenhead incident, I was amazed by my capacity for histrionic extremes. But if instinct told me that I had gone too far that time, that my behaviour was verging on the dangerous, my intelligence told me nothing about the pattern and significance of my hero-worshipping. It did not occur to me that all my heroes were linked by the common theme of disablement, and that this was the quality which invested them with their special charisma. Like any adolescent, I wanted to assume the glow of fame, glamour and achievement, even of genius, and be admired for what I craved but did not possess; unlike most adolescents, I wanted to borrow the essence of those who were wounded in some way, if not actually destroyed. I wanted applause and pity; the power and the excuse of being damaged. I wanted Byron's bad foot as much as his good looks, and if I had been forced to make a choice between them, I would have chosen the foot. Nor did I make any connection between my hero-worship of flawed father figures and my relations with my own father. I did not see – and it would have been a very sophisticated insight for my age if I had done – that my passionate identification with these mutilated heroes owed something to the fearful guilt provoked by my desire to defy and supplant my father.

None of this dawned on me until years later when I undertook a course of psychotherapy. For many weeks I denied that my relationship with my parents was anything but exemplary, and then one night I had an especially vivid dream in which Olivier was my father and my father was Olivier. Thereafter I began to look much more closely at all the 'fathers' in my life.

Self-perception is not an attribute of adolescence; it comes later, if at all, and then only creepingly and by dint of considerable effort. I did nevertheless achieve occasional flashes of understanding, usually prompted by a sense that the compulsions which drove my life had to be reined in and brought under control before they tipped me over and spilt my sanity on the road. At some point I realized that my obsession with Brando, for instance, had grown to grotesque proportions, and that anyway there was something undignified and juvenile about hero-worshipping a mere film star. And so, like a masturbator putting aside his pornography for the last time and swearing never to look at another picture, I took my considerable collection of Brando portraits and holy relics into the garden, made a pyre of them and burnt them until nothing but ash remained. It did the trick; I was cured of Brando-worship and never really regretted my drastic solution. True, I replaced him with other heroes, but none whom I worshipped with the same idolatry.

TWELVE

In his *Biographia Literaria* Samuel Taylor Coleridge includes a short chapter bearing the splendid title 'An affectionate exhortation to those who in early life feel themselves disposed to become authors'. Coming from a life-long literary man, his advice is unexpected, for in effect he urges the would-be author to get a proper job and keep writing for his spare time. '*Never pursue literature as a trade*,' he preaches, and the italics are his. However, not long before he wrote the book, Coleridge had gone through the worst crisis of his life, 'a descent into hell', he called it and this perhaps explains his discouraging attitude.

His conception of the ideal life for a writer, which he projects with rosy eloquence, is that of the professional man, who, comfortable in the knowledge that he has done his duty by wife and family in the 'counting house' or 'manufactury', can settle to his desk of an evening and confront the blank page in a relaxed frame of mind. Then his writing implements will appear to be a chain of flowers linking thought with imagination, rather than a chain of iron binding him to material necessity. Among the many advantages such a way of life can apparently bestow on him is a superior chance of happiness in his domestic relations.

All this is as touching as it is startling to read, not least because it is so far removed from Coleridge's own history. I don't know if he had any particular writer in mind as he developed his fantasy, but none of his own circle of writing friends conformed to it. Nevertheless, he recommends the security of a professional career over the drudgery and uncertainty of authorship. The profession he advocates most warmly to the aspirant writer is the Church (now that would have floored my parents!) but he also mentions the law with approval. The arguments he puts forward in favour of a reliable income and a safe existence are exactly the ones any sensible parent would use in trying to dissuade his child from taking up the pen. At all events, they were the ones my own parents used when I first broached the idea of my becoming a writer and not a lawyer.

This crisis did not break until towards the end of my time at Shrewsbury. Before then my writing, such as it was, had posed no formal threat, and my parents had been proud of my small creative achievements. I regularly contributed short stories and poems to the school magazine, and in one spectacular issue I published a whole sequence of poems dedicated to a girl I had fleetingly known, and desperately loved, one summer holiday. It must have been a brilliant work, for I cannot make head or tail of it now. If I occasionally hinted at my ambition to write for money, it was dismissed as youthful nonsense and raised no real anxiety because, as far as my parents knew, I was still going to be a lawyer.

Meanwhile, however, my fantasies of the artistic life were flourishing under the stimulus of new books and new friends. In particular, I had become friendly with Nick Mander, who shared with me a taste for the 1890s, the Impressionists and Paris in the 1920s. Like me, he was an only child destined for a career in the law, but unlike me, he had very well-developed tastes in all sorts of fields I had never thought about – jazz, opera and indeed all forms of music – as well as being familiar with writers, painters and poets whose names were new to me. He was – and still is – exceedingly good company, and we passed many happy afternoons in lewd speculation concerning the secret lives of our heroes. What exactly did Oscar do to Bosie? What positions did the dwarfish Lautrec take up in bed in his brothel, and did his organ really live up to the legendary length claimed for it by one biographer? Did Beardsley have any sex life at all? After our own fashion, we were both voracious for culture, and though we had very different family backgrounds we were both looking to the arts (Nick painted and wrote) to fill out some emptiness at home.

During my last two years at Shrewsbury, while I was one of only two boys studying English literature at A level under the inspiring tutelage of 'Willy' Jones, I wrote more and more, constantly strengthening my vision of myself as an author. I still had not confronted my parents with my repudiation of the law, and the issue did not come to a head until the summer term of our exams. I was required one day to fill in a form nominating the course I hoped to study at university, a form which would then be sent to my parents for their endorsement. Here was the perfect coward's opportunity to tell them without having to face them. With a flourish, I wrote 'Eng. Lit.' in the appropriate box.

It seemed that no sooner was the ink dry than my parents were driving through the school gates, racing to deal with this, the first real crisis of my hitherto blameless adolescence.

Their response to my mutiny might have been less precipitate, and their opposition to my choice of career less strenuous, had my grandfather not been alive, for he exercised a powerful influence over them. Much more than my father, it was he, the judge, who personified the law in my eyes, together with its increasingly irksome connotations.

If I were to paint a portrait of the judge during the period when he made most impact on my life, I would have to show him seated at the big mahogany writing table which stood in the lounge of the hotel where he went to live after my grandmother had died. Here he would spend his mornings writing letters and memoranda in his clear, elegant hand. My picture would show the table piled high with his dictionaries (English, Latin, French), *Who's Who*, *Titles and Forms of Address*, Fowler's *Modern English Usage*, and other reference books which for him were indispensable to composing even the simplest note. Dangling its long black cord, his gold-rimmed monacle would be screwed securely into his right eye socket, which was perfectly arched and recessed as if machined especially for the job. His face was long and thin and somewhat cadaverous, with a fine steep forehead and a large swooping nose which tilted slightly to the left, the deviation I may or may not have inherited. I would add two more touches: a white cotton handkerchief tucked into his jacket sleeve and drooping a little foppishly round his slender wrist, and his most characteristic hallmark, a panatella held trembling between his fastidious lips.

Like everything else he did, the actual lighting of a cigar, especially a Havana, called for an elaborate ceremonial, which was made especially fascinating, at least in my eyes, by the gracefulness of his long, carefully manicured fingers and the heavy liver mottling on the backs of his hands. Like most gourmets, he was also a towering snob, and he reserved his sharpest contempt for those vulgarians who failed to remove the little paper band from their cigars. Whenever he stripped the band off his own cigar, he would throw a meaningful glance at my father, who was notoriously untrustworthy in these all-important matters of etiquette, and another at myself to remind me of my duties as a young gentleman. Finally, after much sniffing, rolling and crackling, he would put the cigar to his delicately pursed lips and light it up. Just as his eye was ideally formed to clasp a monacle, so his lips, though narrow and tremulous, were wonderfully adapted to grip a cigar. Without effort, he could hold a full-sized corona in his mouth and sit for an hour or more, comfortably impaled, while the smoke gathered in sublime banks above his noble cranium.

My grandfather was immensely proud of me, and when his wife died, a loss from which he never really recovered, he transferred some of his old passion for her on to my fifteen-year-old self. Alas, the grandson of whom he would have been so proud was not the person I was becoming; indeed, I was soon finding it difficult even to act out the grandson of his fantasies during our weekly visits for dinner at his hotel. I wanted to please him, or rather I did not want to displease him, but the young man whose identity he held out for me to put on, like one of the tweed jackets he chose so carefully on my behalf, grew ever more tiresome. His fierce pride, instead of boosting my sense of self-importance, became a source of humiliation, as well as a terrible responsibility I did not want and was bound in the end to shirk.

He wanted me to become a little gentleman, a junior version of himself; someone to whom he could entrust the middle-class standards and traditions he had upheld all his life. He wanted me to inherit and maintain his vision of the world. Most of all, he longed for me to preserve a corner of his

Liverpool, the affluent Liverpool of liners, dinner-dances and bridge clubs where he had been happy and made his professional mark. The irony was that with my public-school assumptions, my plummy voice, my dandified taste in clothes and my place at Cambridge, I came very close to living out his dream.

For him, form was far more significant than content, and he had an exceedingly sharp eye for its finer details, a capacity which had done him no harm in his career. I do not know how good a lawyer he was, nor how merciful he was on the bench, but he certainly made justice look impressive; no casting director could have found an actor to play the role of judge more convincingly. It was not sufficient for me merely to be a young gentleman; I also had to dress and behave like one. Respectability, that most odious of qualities in the nose of all teenagers, was what he wished to see exemplified in my manners and clothes.

When he met us at the door of his hotel, he would greet us with unfailing courtesy, taking my mother's coat and asking my father and me if we wanted to 'wash our hands', but all the while I knew that his punctilious eye was inspecting every thread of my appearance. Throughout the meal, he would be warm in his congratulations on my small achievements, but these would count for nothing if my shoes were not shining, if my tie was sloppily tied, or my hair threatening to overlap my collar. He would never criticize me overtly, for he hated direct confrontation, but he would wait for a suitable gap in the conversation to insinuate an oblique reference to my lapse of the moment, a reference often so convoluted that an outsider would never have deciphered it, though it was always squirmingly clear to me. Usually he would tell a story, or rather a parable, illustrating the downfall of an otherwise worthy person who had sealed his fate by neglecting to wear appropriate clothes for the occasion, by showing his ignorance of the correct form by which to address a bishop, by mispronouncing an awkward word, misusing a Latin tag, or committing some other *faux pas* unforgivable in a person of our social position. These homilies were preached in the abstract, as it were, without the moral being drawn openly, but they were always accompanied by an unmistakable look of reproof aimed at the offender, which as often as not was my father rather than me.

The sad thing was that I could not see him for what he was any more than he could see what I was becoming. With the imperceptiveness of youth, I failed to grasp that he was a lonely, unhappy widower who, through no wish of his own, had been left with nobody to lavish his affections on but us, his uneasy family. Nor did I understand his faults, not least because I shared so many of them. I could not have put labels on his snobbishness, his adulation of titles, his stratagems for ensuring that his own rank as a judge was respected, because they were so much a part of my own normality. It did not strike me as odd that when he took us for lunch at the Adelphi Hotel he would tip the head waiter before and not after the meal, for that was the way he had always done it; as far as I knew that was the way everyone else did it too. His method, incidentally, was most effective, for the anticipatory tip – or bribe, to give it its proper name – produced just the results he wanted. Having pocketed his *douceur*, which was always indecently munificent, the head waiter would retreat before us, almost on his knees, and usher us to the judge's favourite table, where we would be waited on with grovelling servility by a small army of waiters and waitresses, all addressing him as 'Your Honour' in ringing tones which were audible throughout the entire dining-room. Far from being embarrassed by this vulgarity, which after all is what it was, I would revel in it, puffing at my Havana with all the over-fed arrogance of one who had never paid a bill in his life.

I think back on him now with guilt, because I did so little to reciprocate his affection; even less than the little that was required of me. I dreaded our weekly dinners at his hotel, those

pathetic rituals which came to comprise his family life, and I
resented the many kind, if eccentric, gestures he made towards
me, accepting them with an ill grace and giving nothing in
return. I coud not see that the peculiarities of his behaviour –
the signing of his letters as '*avus*' (Latin for grandfather); the
unreadable legal encyclopaedias he compiled for me, copying
their entries out of other encyclopaedias; his eternal fretting
over my clothes, my accent, my manners – were more than
merely autocratic; they were his way of trying to draw me into
his world, of revealing to me the things that gave him pleasure
and satisfaction.

For these reasons he was, I believe, more disappointed than
my father when I proposed to renounce the law. He loved the
law for its own sake, with a passion my father had never felt.
He loved its pageantry, its ceremonial, its history and sacred
rites. But it was just this devotion to pomp and circumstance,
as I saw it, which repelled me and seemed to offer nothing but
manacles to restrain the imagination. He became the living
embodiment of those bourgeois whom my adventurous Aes-
thetes had loved to outrage. His code of behaviour, indeed his
whole way of life, was an oppressive regime of which I was the
single victim – or so I thought, full as I was of the egomania of
youth. For it is one of the more wretched aspects of that
wretched phenomenon adolescence that the whimsicalities of
old age appear to be menacing and repressive, while the
affection that often redeems them goes unnoticed.

If my grandmother, the judge's wife, had been alive when
the crisis over my career finally broke, at the end of my first
year at Cambridge, she might well have eased his disappointment. Had she been with him, my erratic behaviour would not
have loomed so large in his mind, nor would my desertion of
the law have seemed a betrayal, which in his loneliness was
how he interpreted it. Alive, she had always helped him keep a
sense of proportion, but by then she had been dead for more
than four years, and although her loss was always painfully

fresh to him, her moderating influence went with her to the grave.

And so it was, one balmy summer afternoon, that my parents and I came to be sitting on a bench overlooking the cricket pitch at Shrewsbury. To the leisurely sound of young gentle-men executing elegant strokes, we discussed the hard world beyond and what was to become of me when I entered it.

My parents carefully put forward the arguments in favour of my reading law, and Coleridge himself could not have done a better job. While I had the chance, they insisted reasonably, I should gain a qualification in order to have something to fall back on if my writing career failed. In any case, I was foolish to commit myself to writing before knowing whether I had a real talent for it. And even if I did have a talent, there was no guarantee I would make a decent living. Hardly any writers did, whereas lawyers seldom starved, and with my blue-chip pedigree I stood a better chance than most of positively prospering. They were only asking that I should stick at the law for three years, perhaps five in order to qualify, and then, with a certificate to practise behind me, I could have a go at writing. If I started to make money, well and good, I could forget the law and carry on; if not, at least I would have the option of returning to a secure profession. A degree in English Literature, on the other hand, was a passport to nowhere, a qualification for nothing. The alternative to their common-sense plan was painted by my mother in gruesome colours: confined to some garret, I would rot in failure and discomfort – and I did like my creature comforts – until at last I would hit rock bottom and be driven to take up teaching, a fate she evidently regarded as somewhat more ignominious than becoming a lavatory attendant.

Apart from this last argument, which did seem a little incongruous in view of the value they had placed on my education, everything they said was not only logical and sensible, but also sympathetically put. They begged me to see reason and change my mind.

And of course I did, though not because they had convinced me. In fact, nothing they said made any impact on me. Three years indeed! That was a lifetime, and five years was twice a lifetime. As for failure and poverty, the first was inconceivable and I had no fear of the second, since I knew nothing about it except that it was something Whistler and the rest had dismissed as a mere inconvenience. No, I conceded simply because I lacked the emotional strength to resist. I took the dissembler's way out and agreed, while secretly promising myself that I would re-fight the battle another day, on more favourable ground.

EPILOGUE

The following year I went up to Cambridge, to Trinity Hall, the law college, which is handily situated adjacent to the Law Library. One look at that Lubyanka of learning was enough to revive all my misgivings. As I stepped out of my college gate on the first morning of my first term and saw the gleaming white edifice towering above me like some unscalable alp I also saw the cautionary figure of my grandfather. I saw his wig and monacle, his fussing and tutting, his dried-up mind, his 'writing' and his terror of offending the high priest of etiquette. There was the temple of the law, and there too was what the law had done to one of its most faithful servants. Even if I had never heard of Oscar Wilde or art for art's sake, I think I would still have shunned that building, for fear of becoming the grandson of my grandfather's hopes.

I did not at this point have the courage to reopen the battle with my parents. But nor did I have the urge to write. Though yet convinced of my genius, I had somehow lost my schoolboy compulsion to put my ideas on paper, and so I neither wrote nor studied, but relapsed instead into gilded idleness, spending with a carefree hand the savings my mother had amassed so frugally on my behalf. For the first time I joined the distinguished ranks of the overdrawn, and was probably the first Harrison to do so in a hundred years. I overspent as only the young can, blithely confident of a solvent tomorrow.

The same happy disregard for reality sustained my academic expectations: lectures went unattended, books went unread, essays went unwritten, and tutorials were dodged or fudged. The system was lax, being based on the erroneous principle that we were now men, not boys, and I was quick to take advantage of it. I became a foppish layabout.

In the event, I was lucky not to be sent down, and I owe my salvation to the kindliness of Graham Storey, my tutor. He made it possible for me to switch courses at the last possible moment and take up English Literature. While this move effectively brought my legal career to a halt, it did not make me a writer, far less a genius. For nearly ten years after coming down I held a variety of jobs in publishing, a semi-profession which in my parents' eyes at least had the virtue of paying a salary and offering prospects of promotion. In 1975 I abandoned even the dubious security of publishing and with the help of my intrepid wife did at last become a writer, in name and practice. Since then I have fulfilled many of the glummer prophecies made by my parents that summer afternoon at Shrewsbury, but I have also fulfilled a few of my own.

I am a parent myself now, of two children, and engaged in a new round of trivial disputes which as yet are still amicable. I do not know what my reaction will be when my children confront me with their hare-brained schemes for life, as they assuredly will. I cannot decide which I would frown upon more, the idea of their becoming something pennilessly artistic, or something lucrative and respectable. I only hope I will have the wisdom to keep my mouth shut – except to wish them well.

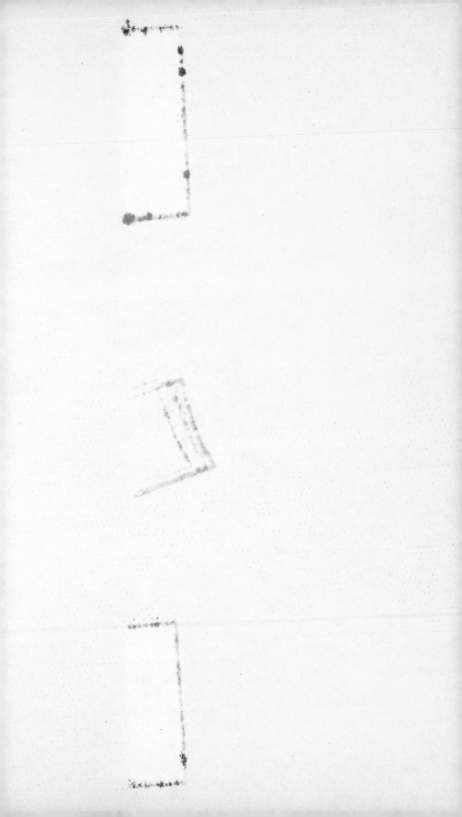

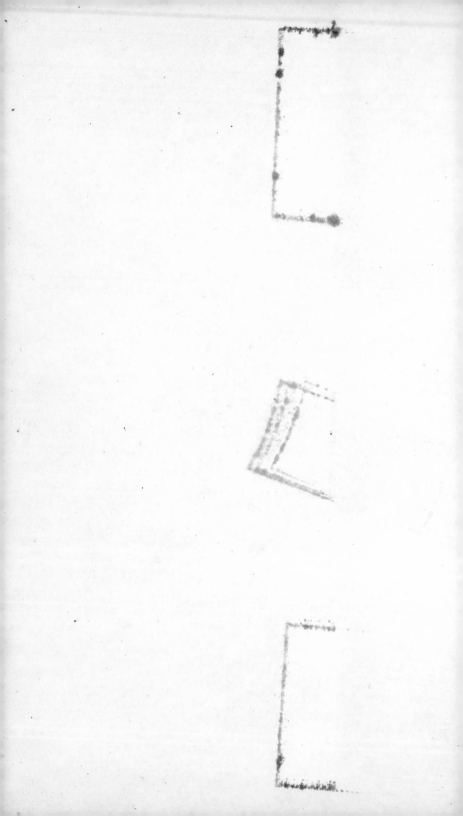